Prayers *for* Occasions

David Adam
Nick Fawcett
Gerald O'Mahony
Susan Sayers
Ray Simpson

Compiled by Sue Cowper

Augsburg Books

MINNEAPOLIS

Prayers compiled from:

1000 Prayers for Public Worship – David Adam
2000 Prayers for Public Worship – Nick Fawcett
Prayers for All Seasons, Books 1 and 2 – Nick Fawcett
A Thousand and One Prayers – Gerald O'Mahony
1500 Prayers for Public Worship – Susan Sayers
His Complete Celtic Prayers – Ray Simpson

PRAYERS FOR OCCASIONS

© Copyright 2013 David Adam, Nick Fawcett, Gerald O'Mahony,
Susan Sayers and Ray Simpson.
Original edition published in English under the title PRAYERS FOR OCCASIONS by
Kevin Mayhew Ltd, Buxhall, England.

Cover image: © iStock 2020: Single woman walking on the hill during sunset by NiseriN
Cover design: Emily Drake

Print ISBN: 978-1-5064-6017-8

About the authors

DAVID ADAM was the Vicar of Lindisfarne, off the Northumbrian coast, for thirteen years until he retired in March 2003. His work involved ministering to thousands of pilgrims and other visitors. He is the author of many inspiring books on spirituality and prayer, and his Celtic writings have rekindled a keen interest in our Christian heritage.

NICK FAWCETT was brought up in Southend-on-Sea, Essex, and trained for the Baptist ministry at Bristol and Oxford, before serving churches in Lancashire and Cheltenham. He subsequently spent three years as a chaplain with the Christian movement Toc H, before focusing on writing and editing, which he continues with today, despite wrestling with cancer. He lives with his wife, Deborah, and two children – Samuel and Kate – in Wellington, Somerset, worshipping at the local Anglican church. A keen walker, he delights in the beauty of the Somerset and Devon countryside around his home, his numerous books owing much to the inspiration he unfailingly finds there.

GERALD O'MAHONY was born in Wigan, Lancashire. He joined the Society of Jesus (the Jesuits) at the age of 18, and was ordained priest aged 30. Gerald was a school teacher for four years, before being invited to join the team of advisers in religious education for the Archdiocese of Liverpool. Ten years on he joined another team, as retreat giver and writer in Loyola Hall Jesuit Spirituality Centre, Rainhill, near Liverpool, where he has lived and worked happily ever since. He is the author of twenty-four books, many of which have been published by Kevin Mayhew.

SUSAN SAYERS is the author of many popular resource books for the church. Through the conferences and workshops she is invited to lead, she has been privileged to share in the worship of many different traditions and cultures. A teacher by profession, she was ordained a priest in the Anglican Church and, before her retirement, her work was divided between the parish of Westcliff-on-Sea, the local women's prison, writing, training days and retreats.

RAY SIMPSON is a Celtic new monastic for tomorrow's world, a lecturer, consultant, liturgist, and author of some 30 books. He is the founding guardian of the international Community of Aidan and Hilda and the pioneer of its e-studies programmes. He is an ordained member of the Christian church and lives on the Holy Island of Lindisfarne. His website is www.raysimpson.org

Contents

Advent

1   Lord Jesus Christ,
    we have come to worship you in this glad season of Advent,
    a season of expectation,
    of celebration,
    and, above all, of preparation.
    We come now, because we want to be ready –
    ready to give thanks for your coming,
    to recognise the ways you come to us now,
    and to welcome you when you come again.
    Open our hearts as we worship you,
    so that all we share may give us a deeper understanding of
    this season
    and a fuller experience of your love.
    In your name we ask it.   *Nick Fawcett*

2   Help us, Lord, in all our preparations for Christmas –
    the writing of cards, buying of presents,
    wrapping of gifts, decorating the home –
    to make ready for you,
    preparing ourselves in heart and mind to worship you afresh
    and welcome you more fully into our lives,
    so that when the day of your coming finally dawns,
    we may be ready to greet you and celebrate a banquet,
    not at our table,
    but yours.   *Nick Fawcett*

3   Lord Jesus Christ,
    teach us to anticipate your return
    by preparing the way for your coming;
    to catch a glimpse of your kingdom
    through living by its values today.
    Live in us now,
    so that the day may come
    when we live with you and all your people
    for all eternity,
    your will complete and your promise fulfilled.
    In your name we ask it.   *Nick Fawcett*

4 Loving God,
   we praise you that the light which dawned
   in the life of Zechariah and Elizabeth,
   that transformed the future for Mary and Joseph,
   and that lit up the sky on the night of the Saviour's birth,
   continues to shine today.
   We thank you for the new beginning you have brought in
   our lives,
   and the light that continues to guide us.
   Teach us to walk in that light day by day,
   and so may each moment be a new dawn,
   a new beginning,
   rich in promise and filled by your love,
   through Jesus Christ our Lord.   *Nick Fawcett*

5 Lord Jesus Christ,
   we thank you for all those who prepared the way for
   your coming,
   whether long ago in Bethlehem
   or in countless hearts since that day.
   We think especially of John the Baptist,
   remembering his courage to speak the truth no matter what
   the cost,
   his readiness to point away from himself and towards
   your light,
   his willingness to live in such a way
   that everything he did testified to the truth of his message
   in a manner that words alone could never do.
   Help us to prepare your way in turn,
   witnessing to your renewing power
   and demonstrating your compassion,
   so that the hearts of many may be made ready to receive you
   and to respond to your grace.
   In your name we ask it.   *Nick Fawcett*

6 Lord Jesus Christ,
   we know and love the message of Christmas so well,
   perhaps too well –
   for we have heard and celebrated it so many times
   and can assume we have understood all it has to say to us.

Save us from that danger,
and help us to reflect on what your coming means
for us,
for others,
for all;
for yesterday,
today
and tomorrow.
Speak to us now,
through readings,
through music,
through prayer,
through your Spirit at work within us.
Speak through all we shall share together,
nurturing our faith,
strengthening our commitment
and expanding our love for you and for all.
In your name we ask it.   *Nick Fawcett*

7   Gracious God,
    we praise you for this season of Advent,
    this time for rejoicing and celebration,
    praise and worship,
    exulting in your goodness.
    We praise you for coming in Christ,
    bringing in a new kingdom
    and anticipating an era of peace and justice
    when the poor will have plenty,
    the hungry be fed,
    and the lowly be lifted up.
    We praise you that you want us to be a part of that,
    not just to share in it but also to play a part in bringing it
    to pass.
    Forgive us that we sometimes lose sight of your purpose
    and underestimate your greatness.
    Open our eyes to the breadth of your love,
    the wonder of your mercy and the extent of your goodness,
    and so may we give you the worship and adoration that is
    due to you,
    this and every day,
    through Jesus Christ our Lord.   *Nick Fawcett*

8 Loving God,
the great festival of Christmas is drawing nearer
and we are busy preparing for it –
choosing presents,
writing cards,
planning get-togethers,
buying food –
so much that has become an accepted and expected part of
this season.
Yet, in all the bustle, we so easily forget what matters most:
responding to the gift of your Son.
Forgive us for relegating Jesus to the periphery of our
celebrations
rather than placing him at the centre where he belongs;
for doing so much to prepare for Christmas on the surface
yet so little to make ourselves ready within.
Open our hearts to welcome the living Christ into our lives,
and so may we rejoice in his love,
not just at Christmas, but always.
In his name we ask it.   *Nick Fawcett*

9 Gracious God,
reminded at this season of your awesome gift in Christ,
we want to respond,
to offer something in return as a sign of our gratitude
for all you have done and continue to do.
We would bring you our worship –
not just well-intentioned thoughts and words
but our wholehearted adoration and joyful thanksgiving.
We would bring you our lives –
not just token deeds or outward show,
but hearts consecrated to your service,
embodying your love for all,
your care and compassion for everything you have made.
Receive, then, this time set aside for you
as a small yet sincere way of acknowledging your goodness,
and through it equip us to live as your people
this and every day.   *Nick Fawcett*

10   Redeemer God,
as we prepare to celebrate the birth of your Son,
speak through the singing of hymns,
the reading of Scripture,
the preaching of your word,
the offering of prayers –
these and so much more.
Break through all that separates us from you and him:
over-familiarity,
indifference,
self-will,
disobedience,
narrowness of vision,
weakness of resolve.
Move among us through your Spirit –
inspiring,
instructing,
revealing,
renewing –
so that we may be equipped to worship
and serve you.   *Nick Fawcett*

11   Almighty God,
we recall at this joyful season how,
through her willingness to hear your word
and commit herself to your service,
you were able to use Mary to fulfil your purpose,
entering our world,
inaugurating your kingdom
and bringing closer that day when sorrow and suffering,
darkness and death will be no more.
Help us, then, as we gather now to worship,
to hear your word
and to respond with similar obedience,
prepared to be used as you see fit.
Through our discipleship,
weak and feeble though it might be,
may your grace be revealed,
your love made known
and your world enriched.   *Nick Fawcett*

12 Lord Jesus Christ,
   born to Mary,
   coming to our world through her,
   be born afresh in us
   that we might be born again through you.
   Touch now this time of worship
   that the message of your birth,
   so familiar and well loved,
   will speak afresh with new power and clarity,
   thrilling our hearts
   and filling us with joy and gratitude.
   Draw close to us now,
   that through welcoming you into our lives
   and opening ourselves once more to your renewing power
   you may reach out through us to the world,
   bringing hope and healing, light and life,
   to the glory of your name.   *Nick Fawcett*

13 Father, may this time of preparing for Christmas
   be a simple time of remembering,
   rather than a celebration of money.
   We ask this through Christ our Lord,
   who came to us poor.   *Gerald O'Mahony*

14 Mary and Joseph had no choice
   but to go to Bethlehem;
   Bethlehem was where Caesar wanted them.
   But Bethlehem was also where God wanted them.
   May we too live our lives in your Providence,
   dear God.   *Gerald O'Mahony*

15 We pray to accept the truth of where we are,
   and to move forward from there,
   seeing the hand of your Providence, dear God,
   leading us to where you want us to be,
   tomorrow.   *Gerald O'Mahony*

16 Father in heaven,
We know from your Son that we cannot serve you
and money.
Please make sure that this Christmas,
inspired by the example of Jesus
we will serve only you, not money. *Gerald O'Mahony*

17 God our Father, may each coming of Christmas
make us more eager to do good,
while we still have time. *Gerald O'Mahony*

18 The story of the first Christmas
is one of outward turmoil, inward peace,
in spite of all the obstacles.
Dear God, may we too trust in your Providence.
Gerald O'Mahony

19 God in heaven, you want all nations
to come streaming to your house and home.
May we not simply rejoice in our own invitation,
but do all we can
to invite others to come with us,
who still do not know your name. *Gerald O'Mahony*

20 Jesus, your mother Mary in her simplicity and sincerity
was ready for your coming into our world.
We pray silently to be made ready for you to come again,
and for all our special needs. *Gerald O'Mahony*

21 The Christmas story makes us reflect
how it should be in families,
each looking out for the other.
Holy Spirit of God, make our own families
to be a place where we feel at home. *Gerald O'Mahony*

22 Heavenly Father,
during this Advent season
we thank you for feeding us
in body, mind and spirit. *Susan Sayers*

23   The world moves round into the light of the day
and we thank you, Father, that we are alive in it.
In this Advent season of watching and waiting,
keep us attentive to you, throughout the day,
ready to listen, ready to learn and ready to love. *Susan Sayers*

24   Another Advent has begun.
Lord our God,
lead us in the way of truth and love,
kindness and mercy.
As we get ready for Christmas,
may we learn more about loving you
and loving one another.
Give us courage to keep asking
the big questions about life and death,
knowing that you are in our past, our present and
all our future.
You know us completely and you love us
completely.
Thank you, Lord God, for making us,
and for coming to be born among us as a baby.
May we worship you with our whole lives.   *Susan Sayers*

25   Through the generations
your people waited in hope and expectation.
Now in the darkness of this Advent night
we re-live that waiting with them,
re-live that small bright hope
as it brightens into the full glory
'as of the only begotten of the Father –
full of grace and truth'.
Amen. Come, Lord Jesus!   *Susan Sayers*

26   As we share in Mary and Elizabeth's joy
at the coming of our Saviour,
we quieten and still ourselves
in the presence of you, God.
Heavenly Father, we can only marvel
at the way you are happy to work with us.
We want you to know
that we are willing to be used.   *Susan Sayers*

Christmas

27   Jesus Christ, you have come
to lift us into the fullness of your kingdom.
You, dear Lord, have become human
that we may share in your divinity.
You have come to live among us
that we may be your friends.
We give you thanks for Christmas,
for the gift of your presence and yourself.   *David Adam*

28   Every day can be a Christmas day,
for the Lord comes to us as he came to Bethlehem.
He seeks to be born in us;
he wants us to come to him like the shepherds;
he wants to live in and work through us;
he comes eternally and seeks room in our lives,
for the Lord comes to us as he came to Bethlehem.
   David Adam

29   We give thanks that our Lord
was born into an ordinary family
and lived in an ordinary home.
We ask your blessing
upon all our loved ones and friends this Christmas:
may we know your presence in our joys and celebrations.
We remember all who have to spend this Christmas
away from their homes and loved ones.   *David Adam*

30   Lord Jesus, you have come among us,
to share in our lives and to let us share in yours.
As you give yourself to us today,
help us to give ourselves to you.   *David Adam*

31   We give thanks for all who celebrate Christmas,
all who are worshipping in churches and in their homes,
all who acknowledge Jesus in their midst.   *David Adam*

32   Father, we rejoice and sing,
      for you love us with a great love.
      We give thanks to you
      for the coming of our Lord Jesus Christ into our world
      and into our lives.
      Let us enjoy your presence with us,
      and the love you offer to us in Jesus our Lord. *David Adam*

33   May the humility of the shepherds,
      the perseverance of the wise men,
      the joy of the angels,
      be God's gifts to us and to people everywhere
      this Christmas time.
      And may the blessing of the Christ child
      be upon us always.   *David Adam*

34   We ask your blessing
      upon all who do not celebrate this Christmas.
      We remember all who will be homeless or lonely
      and all who are poor or deeply in debt.
      We pray that our homes
      may be places of love and peace
      where you, Christ, are welcome.
      May we know that in the coming of others to us
      you also come and seek our love.   *David Adam*

35   We give thanks for our homes
      and the friends with whom we will celebrate
      this Christmas.
      We remember absent friends and loved ones.
      We remember all who are lonely
      or feel rejected at this time.   *David Adam*

36   Loving God,
      you have come to us in Christ.
      So now we come to you,
      to offer our worship,
      to hear your word
      and to reflect on your love.

Help us through all we share today
to hear the story of Christmas speaking to us as though for
the first time.
May familiar and well-loved words take on new meaning,
so that we may share the elation of Mary,
the excitement felt by the shepherds,
and the wonder experienced by the wise men.
May what was news of great joy for them,
bring joy likewise to us,
this and every day,
through Jesus Christ our Lord.   *Nick Fawcett*

37 Sovereign God,
though we have heard it so many times before,
and though the words of readings and carols we will
share today
are so familiar we know them almost back to front,
grant that through the worship we bring you
our hearts may thrill again to the good news of Christ,
and our spirits soar at the message of his coming.
Grant us new insights and deeper understanding,
so that our faith may be enriched and our joy increased
as we celebrate the great gift of your Son –
glad tidings yesterday,
today
and every day.   *Nick Fawcett*

38 Lord Jesus Christ,
like the shepherds of old
we come with hearts ablaze to celebrate your birth,
to kneel in wonder,
to offer our thanksgiving
and to respond personally to you.
May we, like them, thrill to the good news of your coming,
and go on our way rejoicing,
making known to those we meet
everything we have found to be true in you.
In your name we pray.   *Nick Fawcett*

39 Lord Jesus Christ,
you were born so that you might die.
You took on our humanity
so that you might experience also our mortality.
Only through identifying yourself so totally with us
could you bridge the gap that separates us from God.
You showed us the way of love,
and you followed it through to the end.
You proclaimed forgiveness,
and you paid the price to make it possible.
In life and in death, you testified to the grace of the Father,
and his purpose for all the world.
Help us, as we celebrate again your birth,
never to forget that this was just the beginning of the story.
As we greet you now as the child of Bethlehem,
so let us greet you also as the crucified Saviour
and the risen Lord,
and may we offer you,
this and every day,
our joyful worship
in grateful praise.   *Nick Fawcett*

40 How much time, Lord,
will we make for you this Christmas?
How much time,
before, during and after the celebrations,
to reflect on your love?
Will we put you at the centre of our celebrations,
the heart of our lives,
or relegate you to the margins,
include you almost as an afterthought?
Forgive us, for all too often,
at Christmas or otherwise,
we have time for just about everything . . .
except you.   *Nick Fawcett*

41 Gracious God,
we thank you that you have given us good news in Christ,
a message that has thrilled generations across the years,
uplifting,

encouraging,
challenging
and renewing.
We thank you for the way that message has spoken to us,
shown to be glad tidings in so many ways.
Yet we confess that we sometimes lose our initial sense
of awe
and wonder,
and no longer feel the urge to respond to your love
as powerfully as we once did.
Forgive us for becoming casual and complacent in our faith,
failing to make time to worship,
and forgetting the need to nurture our relationship with you.
Speak to us again,
meet us through the living Christ,
and open our hearts to the renewing touch of your
Holy Spirit.
So may we catch again the sense of urgency felt by
the shepherds
as they rushed to Bethlehem,
and may the wonder of your love burn within us each day,
to your glory.   *Nick Fawcett*

42   Loving God,
     we thank you for the great truth at the heart of this season –
     your coming to our world in Christ.
     We praise you that you go on coming,
     day after day,
     not just to others but also to us,
     meeting and working within us through your Holy Spirit.
     Forgive us everything that obstructs your coming –
     all the trivia and irrelevancies with which we fill our lives
     at the cost of time for you;
     all the cares, doubts and unbelief
     that prevent us sometimes from even glimpsing
     your presence.
     Come afresh now,
     and break through all the barriers in our lives,
     so that we may know you more nearly by our side
     and draw yet closer to you than we have ever been before.

Speak your word,
grant your guidance,
confer your power
and fill us with your love,
so that we may serve you as faithfully
as you have served us in Christ.
In his name we ask it.   *Nick Fawcett*

43 Gracious God,
we thank you for the glorious message of this season:
the glad tidings of great joy,
ever old yet ever new.
We thank you for the faith of Mary,
the commitment of Joseph,
the message of the angels
and the response of the shepherds –
the way you changed their lives that day in Bethlehem.
Above all, though,
we thank you that you have changed our lives too;
that the good news these heard and responded to long ago
is news still today –
as special now as then,
and for us as much as anyone!
Teach us never to forget that wonderful truth;
never to overlook the fact that you have come to us in Christ.
May that knowledge burn brightly in our hearts,
a constant source of joy and inspiration,
whatever life may bring.
In the name of Christ, we ask it.   *Nick Fawcett*

44 Remind us, Lord,
that after the stable came a cross,
after birth, death,
after celebration, sacrifice,
and after pleasure, pain,
each bound by a single stem:
the wonder of your love.
Help us to rejoice in all that this season means,
not just in part,
but in full.   *Nick Fawcett*

45 Teach us, Lord,
to put you at the centre of Christmas,
so that it may transform our lives –
the things we do,
the way we think,
the people we are,
the church we long to be –
each touched by your presence
and made new by your love.   *Nick Fawcett*

46 Living God,
we remember today
how shepherds responded to the message of the angels –
how they hurried to Bethlehem
and found the baby lying in a manger,
and how afterwards they went on their way,
sharing what they had seen and heard.
Teach us to share our experience of Christ in turn.
Help us to understand that your coming through him
is good news for everyone,
and that you want us to help make that known.
Enable us, then, to live each day with joy in our hearts
and wonder in our eyes
as we share the love you have shown us
and make known the great thing you have done in Christ.
In his name we ask it.   *Nick Fawcett*

47 The world Jesus was born into
was the world we know.
Thank you for being prepared
to face the dangers and risks
of human mistakes and sin
in order to save us.   *Susan Sayers*

48 Many of us will be celebrating
with our families and friends.
We invite you to join us in all the festivities,
and ask you to teach us true loving.   *Susan Sayers*

49 As we celebrate Christmas,
when the Word of God became flesh,
we pray for the Church, the Body of Christ.
May we be so filled with God's loving life
that our actions touch the world with hope
which lasts even when Christmas decorations
are put away.   *Susan Sayers*

50 Lord, we recognise our great need of your grace,
and give you thanks and praise
for making possible what would otherwise
be impossible.   *Susan Sayers*

51 Thank you, Lord Jesus,
for coming to share our human lives.
Dying, you destroyed our death.
Rising, you restored our life.
Lord Jesus, come again in glory.   *Susan Sayers*

52 Here I offer you, Lord Jesus,
all my preparations for Christmas.
Teach me more about giving
and more about receiving.
Realign my priorities
in tune with your will,
and enable me to see more clearly
how best to celebrate your coming
as our Lord and Saviour.   *Susan Sayers*

53 Lord God, thank you for healing me
with the blessing of your forgiveness.
Thank you for your generous, shining love
that changes crusted lives and broken spirits.
Thank you that you love us as we are
and are happy to enlist our help
in the lighting of dark places,
bringing hope and joy.
Blessed be God for ever.   *Susan Sayers*

54 *A grace to say at your Christmas dinner*
Lord Jesus, born in Bethlehem
on the first Christmas Day,
welcome to this meal with us.
We give thanks to God for food on the table
and for the love and fellowship we share.
As we eat and drink to celebrate Christmas,
may we know your love in our hearts.   *Susan Sayers*

55 Father, as we celebrate the birth of Jesus, your Word,
we thank you with our whole heart.
The bells and lights and presents and decorations
in church and in our homes
express our thanks to you, Lord,
for coming into the world in person.   *Susan Sayers*

56 As Christmas brings together
family members and friends,
and we make contact with those we seldom meet,
may all our relationships be nourished
with love and forgiveness,
and may we value one another more.   *Susan Sayers*

57 We pray that the light of the world
may shine so brightly in our lives
that other people notice it
and are attracted to you
by the way we live and love.   *Susan Sayers*

58 Jesus, proclaimed by angels;
light up our darkness.
Jesus, worshipped by shepherds;
light up our darkness.
Jesus, adored by wise men;
light up our darkness.
Jesus, God who is with us now;
light up our darkness.   *Ray Simpson*

59 Jesus Christ, Son of glory,
who for love comes among us,
bless to us this day of joy.
Open to us heaven's generous gates.
Strengthen our hope.
Revive our tired souls
till we sing the joys of your glory
with all the angels of heaven.
Hold also those who are sleeping rough,
those who feel shut out of society,
those who are cold and hungry,
and these we name before you now. *Ray Simpson*

60 Child of Glory, Child of Mary,
at your birth you were proclaimed the Prince of Peace.
You came to remove the wall
that divides one people from another;
may walls of hostility and fear come tumbling down.
Ray Simpson

61 O Saviour Christ,
you existed before the world began.
You came to save us and we are witnesses of your goodness.
You became a tiny child in a cot
showing us the simplicity of our parents' love.
You chose Mary as your mother
and raised all motherhood to a divine vocation.
May all mothers be bearers of life and grace
to their husbands, their children
and to all who come to their homes. *Ray Simpson*

Lent

62 Blessed are you, Lord God of our salvation;
to you be praise and glory for ever.
As we rejoice this day
in the triumphant entry into Jerusalem,
may we too be willing to walk the way of the cross.

By our lives may we witness to you
as our Lord and King
and declare your saving love to the world.   *David Adam*

63   Blessed are you, Lord God of all creation.
     You have created us out of your love and for your love.
     Help us to welcome you with songs of 'Hosanna',
     knowing that you are our strength and our shield.
     Help us to welcome Christ our Lord into our lives
     as our Lord and Saviour.   *David Adam*

64   Blessed are you, Lord Jesus,
     for you are our Saviour.
     As you were welcomed into Jerusalem,
     may we welcome you into our homes and our lives.
     Let our lives sing Hosannas to you,
     that we may be full of your praise.
     As we carry palm crosses
     may we know the great sacrifice of love
     that you made for us,
     Jesus our Lord and King.   *David Adam*

65   Blessed are you, Lord our God,
     for you have redeemed us
     by the offering of your Son upon the cross.
     Through his death you destroy death
     and open to us the kingdom of heaven.
     As we seek to welcome Jesus into our lives
     with cries of 'Hosanna',
     and as we walk the way of the cross,
     keep us ever mindful of your love and your peace.
             David Adam

66   Lord God, whose Son Jesus Christ
     rode into Jerusalem as the Messiah,
     to suffer and die,
     bless these palms
     that they may be to us a sign of his victory.

May we who hold them
always accept him as our King
until we rejoice in the kingdom
where he reigns with you and the Holy Spirit,
now and for ever.   *David Adam*

67 Lord Jesus, as you approached Jerusalem
the crowds welcomed you with loud 'Hosannas';
may we welcome you into our homes and our hearts
as our Saviour.   *David Adam*

68 Lord God,
we hold these palm crosses as signs
of Jesus our King riding into Jerusalem as the Messiah
and of his suffering and dying on the cross.
Bless these palms that they may be to us
a sign of his victory and of your eternal love.
May we who hold them
always accept him as our King
until we rejoice in the kingdom
where he reigns with you and the Holy Spirit,
now and for ever.   *David Adam*

69 God, we thank you for your redeeming love.
You have sent your Son to be our Saviour.
You have rescued us from darkness and death
and given us eternal life.
To you, Lord, be praise and glory for ever.   *David Adam*

70 Lord God, we thank you
for the coming of Christ into the world
and sharing in our troubles.
We rejoice in your saving power
and in the promise of life eternal.
We pray for all who seek to walk the way of the cross.
We remember pilgrims in Jerusalem
and all who keep this Holy Week.
We ask your blessing
upon all Christians who are facing persecution
and rejection at this time.   *David Adam*

71   Lord Jesus, who walked the way of the cross
      and gave yourself willingly for us,
      help us to be generous in our living
      and to give ourselves to you.   *David Adam*

72   Lord Jesus Christ,
      speak to us of the new life you have made possible
      through your stupendous sacrifice,
      your willingness to surrender all.
      Unfold to us the true nature of discipleship –
      what it means to love and follow you –
      and help us, by your grace, to respond,
      dying to self and rising to new life with you,
      so that all we do and are may be by your power,
      in your service
      and to your glory.   *Nick Fawcett*

73   Sovereign God,
      we would draw close and learn of you,
      so that we might know, love and serve you better.
      Receive, then, the worship we bring
      and meet us through it,
      speaking your word,
      offering your guidance,
      imparting your strength
      and granting your mercy.
      Give us a clearer understanding of your will
      and help us to recognise everything in our lives
      that conspires against it;
      that leads us astray,
      separating us from you and one another.
      Grant us grace to resist temptation,
      and to walk in your way,
      now and always.   *Nick Fawcett*

74   Lord Jesus Christ,
      we praise you for your ministry,
      your love,
      your faithfulness to your calling.

We thank you for your willingness to face even death itself
so that we might find the true meaning of life.
We thank you for that sense of purpose,
that inner courage,
that deep faith which gave you the strength
to continue on your chosen path
to the very end.
Lord Jesus Christ,
forgive us that having received so much we give so little
in return.
Forgive us that we shy away from sacrifice and self-denial.
Forgive us for taking the easy and less costly way
rather than the way of the cross.
Help us to deny ourselves
and so to find life in all its fullness.
In your name we ask it.

Nick Fawcett

75   Examine us, Lord,
     and know our thoughts.
     Search us,
     and help us to see where we are spiritually weak,
     our faith lacking and our commitment poor.
     Put a new heart and a right spirit within us,
     and, by your grace,
     make us whole.

Nick Fawcett

76   You call us to imitate you, Lord –
     to reflect something of your light and love in our lives,
     but we find it so hard,
     the picture we give to others
     proving a feeble caricature of who and what you are.
     Though we will always fall short,
     help us, we pray,
     to be a little more like Jesus,
     our lives in some way speaking to others of him.

Nick Fawcett

77 Lord,
we talk glibly of sacrifice and self-denial,
when in reality we live almost wholly for our own ends,
unwilling to surrender even a little for you or others.
We daily deny you.
Give us a genuine commitment to Christ that shows itself
in action;
a faith that makes a difference to who and what we are,
unmistakable to all.   *Nick Fawcett*

78 Examine us, Lord,
and show us what's wrong in our lives.
Search us,
and help us to recognise where we go astray.
Teach us to look carefully at who and what we are,
identifying our faults and weaknesses,
and, with your help,
seeking to put them right,
so that, imperfect though we are,
we may approximate more nearly
to what we're meant to be
and what we hunger to become.   *Nick Fawcett*

79 Eternal God,
as we worship you today and throughout this season of Lent,
help us to recognise all that is wrong in our lives,
all that separates us from you and others,
all that obstructs your purpose,
leads us into temptation
and causes us to fall.
Help us, prayerfully and humbly, to examine ourselves
and honestly acknowledge our faults,
not so that we might wallow in self-pity or indulge in
false piety,
but so that we may receive cleansing, healing
and forgiveness –
renewal in body, mind and spirit,
through Jesus Christ our Lord.   *Nick Fawcett*

80 Lord Jesus Christ,
faced with difficult decisions
so often we tell ourselves we have no choice,
that life has pushed us into a corner,
leaving us no alternative as to how to act.
But in our hearts we know that isn't so.
It may be hard, painful or costly,
but finally there is always a right way
if we are prepared to look for it.
Forgive us for all the excuses we make.
Forgive us for the ways we wriggle and squirm
rather than face up to our responsibilities.
Forgive us for all the times we have taken the soft option
rather than the one we know to be right.
Teach us, next time we have to make a choice,
to seek your will,
to listen to your voice
and to respond in faith,
to the glory of your name.   *Nick Fawcett*

81 Almighty and all-seeing God,
we thank you for this season of Lent:
a time to reflect upon our discipleship,
to consider our calling,
to examine ourselves
and to assess the health of our faith.
Help us to be honest in this:
to see ourselves as we really are
with all our weaknesses, ugliness and sinfulness.
Help us to face the things we usually prefer to push aside;
the unpleasant truths we sweep under the carpet,
pretending they are not there.
Help us to come to you now,
acknowledging our faults,
recognising our weaknesses
and receiving your forgiveness,
which alone can make us whole,
through the grace of Christ.   *Nick Fawcett*

82 Gracious God,
  we thank you for the time spent by Jesus in the wilderness,
  tested there to the limit but refusing to be deceived.
  Help us to learn from his example;
  to be awake to temptation and ready to withstand it;
  to make time to hear your voice
  and reflect upon your word.
  Help us to follow you and to do your will,
  regardless of the cost.
  So may we grow closer to you and stronger in our faith.

  Nick Fawcett

83 We remember, Lord God,
  how Jesus had to choose in the wilderness
  between the way of self or others –
  and how he chose the latter,
  knowing it would mean suffering and sacrifice,
  the agony of death on a cross,
  and that once he started out
  there could be no turning back.
  Help us to follow you with similar commitment,
  ready to walk your way to our journey's end.   *Nick Fawcett*

84 Help us to give something up for Lent, Lord,
  not because it's expected or out of empty show
  but to promote our spiritual health.
  Enable us, with your help,
  to cut out whatever undermines our discipleship,
  denying your love and frustrating your purpose;
  whatever, in other words,
  creates a barrier between us,
  preventing us from knowing you
  as we should and could.   *Nick Fawcett*

85 Almighty God,
  teach us what it means to love,
  what it takes to follow you,
  what it costs to serve you,
  and help us to stay true when testing comes,
  choosing your way and walking it faithfully
  with all our heart and mind and soul.   *Nick Fawcett*

86 As we begin this season of Lent
we ask you to remind us of what is important
and what is not;
of where we are wandering away
and what we need to change;
so that by Easter
we will be renewed and strengthened
for your service in the world. *Susan Sayers*

Easter

87 Christ, risen in glory,
scatter the darkness
from your heart and mind
and from the world,
that you may live in the fullness of life
and in awareness of his glorious kingdom.
And the blessing of God Almighty, the Father,
the Son and the Holy Spirit, be upon you now and for ever.
David Adam

88 Lord, as we celebrate your resurrection,
strengthen your Church
to tell the Good News to the whole world.
Bless all who are called to teach and preach
in your name.
In the power of the risen Lord,
may they lead us from darkness
to his glorious light. *David Adam*

89 With the whole Church
throughout the world and in heaven
we rejoice,
for Christ is risen.
Let every Christian rejoice,
let every heart rejoice,
for Christ is risen. *David Adam*

90   Blessed are you, Lord our God.
On the first Easter Day
you raised your Son, Jesus Christ,
triumphant over death, sin and evil.
In his death you have destroyed death
and in his rising to life you have opened to us
the kingdom of heaven.
Blessed are you, Father, Son and Holy Spirit.   *David Adam*

91   May the Christ raised in glory
scatter the darkness from our hearts and minds
and from this world.
May the light of the risen Christ
shine upon us this day and always.
Alleluia, Christ is risen.
He is risen indeed.
Alleluia.   *David Adam*

92   Blessed are you, mighty God,
Creator of light and darkness.
To you be praise and glory for ever.
By the resurrection of your Son to eternal life
you have destroyed the darkness and fear of death.
Radiant life is ours through him who loves us,
Jesus, our Lord and our friend.
Blessed are you, Father, Son and Holy Spirit,
our God for ever and ever.   *David Adam*

93   Blessed are you,
God and Father of our Lord Jesus Christ.
To you be praise and glory for ever.
From the darkness of death
you have raised your Son to eternal life.
Through him death is destroyed,
light conquers darkness,
love defeats hatred
and your redeeming love is offered to us all.
Blessed are you, Lord God, for ever.
Alleluia.   *David Adam*

94 God, we thank you that seeds and bulbs grow in secret
without us seeing them.
We trust they will rise out of the earth.
We thank you for Jesus who,
though crucified, dead and buried,
rose again for us.   *David Adam*

95 Blessed are you, Creator of life and joy.
We give you thanks for the promise of eternal life
offered through the death and resurrection
of your Son, Jesus Christ.
As we rejoice in the gift of this new day
we seek to delight in you and in your great love.
Blessed are you for ever.   *David Adam*

96 Lord, make us aware of your risen presence
in our lives.
May our worship be full of joy and awe.
Give us the courage to go out
to proclaim your love and your saving power. *David Adam*

97 Lord, we are Easter people:
let 'Alleluia' be our song.
We give you thanks and praise
for the resurrection of our Lord Jesus Christ
and for his appearances to his loved ones.
We rejoice with the whole Church
in the joy of the risen Lord.
May we who know the Good News
go and tell others that he is risen.   *David Adam*

98 Blessed are you, Lord our God,
for in your love you sent your Son Jesus Christ
to be our Saviour.
You deliver us from the darkness of sin and death
and open to us the way to eternal life.
Blessed are you, Father, Son and Holy Spirit.
To you be praise and glory for ever.   *David Adam*

99 Glory and honour and blessing be yours,
great and mighty God.
In the resurrection you have destroyed death
and opened to us the gate of glory.
In you are life and life eternal.
We give you thanks and praise for ever and ever.

David Adam

100 Blessed are you, Lord God,
by whose power our Lord Jesus is raised from the dead.
In your presence is life and life eternal.
In your power death is conquered
and the gate to eternal life is opened.
In your presence is the fullness of joy.   *David Adam*

101 Help us today, Lord,
to recognise the awfulness of your death,
the awesomeness of your sacrifice;
to remember how nails pierced your hands and feet,
crushing flesh and bone,
the pain too dreadful to contemplate,
never mind the agony afterwards.
For the immense love that could endure all this,
willingly,
gladly,
for such as us,
receive our heartfelt praise.   *Nick Fawcett*

102 Lord Jesus Christ,
we marvel again today at your astonishing love:
the way you endured the humiliation of Gethsemane,
the agony of the cross
and the darkness of the tomb,
not because you had to
but because you chose to.
We praise you that, despite the jeers and ridicule you faced,
your concern was always for others rather than yourself,
and thus you freely chose the way of humility, service
and self-sacrifice:
the lonely path of the cross.

Above all,
we praise you for your faithfulness to the last –
that though you could so easily have stepped down from
the cross,
you didn't;
and though you could have saved yourself,
you preferred instead to save the world.

Lord Jesus Christ,
however often we hear it,
still we are amazed by the magnitude of your love
and the awesomeness of your sacrifice.
Receive our praise and accept our worship,
for your name's sake.

Nick Fawcett

103   Lord Jesus Christ,
whoever we are,
whatever we have done,
we know it is never too late to respond to your love,
for you are always ready to forgive and forget,
always waiting to pick up the pieces of our lives
and help us start again.
We praise you that this is why you came –
to offer a clean break to everyone who recognises their need;
a new beginning in this life and the life to come –
and, in that assurance, we come now seeking your help
and mercy,
for our sin and weakness is ever before us.

Lord Jesus Christ,
as the thief asked on the cross, so we ask too:
'When you come into your kingdom,
remember me.'

Nick Fawcett

104   Speak afresh, Lord,
to us and your world,
of the cross of Christ and all it continues to mean;
of how he staggered under its weight
and hung on it finally in agony.

However familiar it may be,
save us from taking it for granted
and forgetting the awesome love of which it speaks.

Nick Fawcett

105   Remind us, Lord,
that your cross speaks not just of a single day,
but of every day,
changing every moment and everything.
Help us more fully to understand
and celebrate your grace,
so that it may shape our lives,
now, and always.

Nick Fawcett

106   Lord Jesus Christ,
you suffered so much for our sakes –
pain of mind as well as body:
the pain of waiting for the end,
of mockery and rejection,
of betrayal, denial and misunderstanding,
of flogging and physical blows,
of thorns pressed on to your head
and nails driven into your hands and feet,
of hanging in agony on that cross.

Lord Jesus Christ,
as we celebrate all you have given us,
help us never to forget what it cost you.

Nick Fawcett

107   Lord Jesus Christ,
broken for us,
remind us that the cross was not the end:
that from death came life,
from despair, hope
and from sorrow, joy –
your love bringing new beginnings.
And remind us,
above all,
that this same love is still at work,

here and now today,
able to take broken people,
broken lives,
and make them whole. *Nick Fawcett*

108 Whatever else we grow tired of, Lord,
help us still to celebrate the Good News of Christ –
something to go on getting excited about,
day after day. *Nick Fawcett*

109 Lord Jesus Christ,
for the victory you have won over sin and death,
and the victories you continue to win in our lives,
receive our praise. *Nick Fawcett*

110 Lord Jesus Christ,
we praise you that we can worship you
not simply as the crucified Christ
but as our risen Lord and Saviour.
We praise you that death was not the end but a new beginning,
not simply for you but for us!
We praise you for this time of joy, thanksgiving and rejoicing,
a time that speaks of victory, renewal and hope.
For the great message of Easter
that has spoken to countless people across the years
and that continues to speak to us today,
receive our joyful and grateful worship.
Come among us now, in your risen power,
and send us out to proclaim your name
and live to your glory,
for your name's sake. *Nick Fawcett*

111 Living God,
we praise you for the wonder of Easter –
this day that changed the world for ever!
We rejoice in the victory of Christ:
his triumph over evil,
hatred,
despair,
and even death itself.

Living God,
we praise you for the victory you have won,
and for the assurance it brings that nothing in life or death
can ever separate us from your love;
nothing in heaven or earth defeat your loving purpose for
all the world.
To you be praise and glory,
this day and always.

Nick Fawcett

112   Lord Jesus Christ,
as Mary recognised you in the garden,
as disciples met you on the Emmaus Road,
as the Apostles encountered you standing among them
and as Thomas knelt before you in homage,
his doubts and questions overcome,
so we would meet you now,
our risen Lord and Saviour,
conqueror of evil,
triumphant over death.
We would acknowledge your greatness,
acclaim your love,
salute your victory
and celebrate the new life you have given –
the hope, joy, peace and blessing
you have poured into our hearts.
Accept, then, our worship,
and meet us through it.

Nick Fawcett

113   Risen Saviour,
though we have not seen the empty tomb and
folded grave-clothes,
the wounds in your hands and feet,
or your physical presence among us,
yet we believe,
for we have tasted your love,
experienced your power,
known you deep within us through your Holy Spirit
bringing joy, peace and fullness of life.

So we come today, simply to acclaim you,
to bring our worship,
to express our gratitude,
to acknowledge you in praise, wonder and adoration,
as our Lord and our God.   *Nick Fawcett*

114 Lord Jesus Christ,
we celebrate again today your triumph over falsehood
and evil;
the fact that all the attempts to discredit you
and to suppress the truth of your resurrection
came to nothing,
for it was impossible to deny the reality of your presence
in the hearts of those who knew you.
Forgive us that we are not always as truthful as we should be,
slipping so easily into white lies,
or hiding behind half-truths.
Remind us that your truth can set us free,
and so teach us to receive it with joy,
speak it in love and live by it in faith,
trusting in your love that alone will never fail.
In your name we ask it.   *Nick Fawcett*

115 Thank you, Lord,
that you do not leave us alone,
instead drawing alongside us each day.
Thank you that,
just as you met with your followers on the road
and your disciples in the upper room,
so, in Christ, you meet with us in the journey of life,
always there, in your resurrection power,
to guide, protect, comfort and support,
each of us valued as a little child,
chosen and precious to you.   *Nick Fawcett*

116 Lord Jesus Christ,
we thank you for the great message of Easter –
that in what the world counted defeat you won the greatest
of victories.

We praise you for your triumph over evil and death,
and for everything this has meant over the years to so
many people.
Most of all,
we thank you for our own experiences of your
resurrection power –
the times you have brought us victory
over all that stops us living life to the full.
Teach us to live each day in the light of what you have done,
confident that no situation,
however dreadful it may seem,
is finally beyond your power to redeem,
and so may we put our trust in you always,
for this life
and the life to come.   *Nick Fawcett*

117   Help us to remember, Lord,
that Easter is not a holiday but a holy day,
speaking of you and your love in Christ,
his resurrection and the life you promise us in turn.
Wherever we are, then, and whatever we do,
help us to remember what this season is ultimately about,
and to make space for you as well as for us.   *Nick Fawcett*

118   Lord Jesus Christ,
you came to bring us life in all its fullness;
to offer hope beyond the grave.
Teach us that death is not the end, but a new beginning –
the gateway to life everlasting.
And may that confidence shape our attitude not only
towards death
but towards life also.
May we live each day in the context not just of the here
and now
but of eternity,
knowing there is nothing in heaven or earth
that shall ever finally be able to separate us from your love.
                                                       Nick Fawcett

119 Lord God,
may we proclaim with joy
your message of hope
for the world;
may our lives,
as well as our worship,
testify to the truth
of the Resurrection;
broaden our vision
of what is possible
through new life in you.

Susan Sayers

Harvest

120 Loving God,
we come this day to praise you,
to celebrate your great goodness.
We come with thanksgiving, joy and wonder,
reminding ourselves of the richness of your creation,
and acknowledging your faithfulness
in providing for all our needs and far beyond!
You have blessed us beyond our deserving:
gladly we rejoice.

For the beauty of the seasons,
the constant cycle of day and night,
and the vital gifts of rain and sunshine,
we praise you.

For the miracle of growth,
the wonder of life,
and the incredible variety of harvest,
we bring you our thanksgiving.

Receive then our worship,
accept our offerings,
bless our celebration,
and fill us with thankfulness for all you have given.

Nick Fawcett

121 Lord of life,
we gather this day to praise you,
to acknowledge you as Creator of heaven and earth,
to thank you for your faithful provision,
and to celebrate the constant cycle of the seasons,
of day and night,
seed-time and harvest.
Day by day,
year by year,
we see your hand at work,
we marvel at the beauty of your design,
and we rejoice in all you have given.
We praise you for this vast and awesome universe
in which you have placed us,
this world in which we live,
and this country in which we have been born –
so many reasons to count our blessings,
so much to thank you for.
We thank you for the harvest which surrounds us today,
for the many places from which it has come,
for the toil which has made it possible,
and for your hand which ultimately lies behind it.

Lord of life,
we recognise again your goodness,
we remember once more how fortunate we are,
and we celebrate the bountiful provision of your creation.
Gladly we come,
with thankful hearts and joyful worship.
In the name of Christ.   *Nick Fawcett*

122 What harvest do we show in our lives, Lord?
In what ways do we bear fruit,
reflecting the work of your Spirit within us?
Too often we fail to practise what we preach,
our discipleship proving barren.
Reach out in mercy,
and nurture the seeds you have sown within us,
so that they may truly grow and flourish,
to your glory.   *Nick Fawcett*

123 Gracious God,
we have so much to thank you for,
your creation so rich
and the resources you have given us so many,
and yet we all too rarely show our gratitude.
We take your blessings for granted,
complaining about what we haven't got
instead of rejoicing in what we have.
We are not only ungrateful but irresponsible,
squandering what you have given,
frittering away the earth's treasures
with no thought of tomorrow.

We are part of a world which wantonly pollutes
and knowingly wastes,
and we have done little if anything about it,
preferring a life of comfort
to the sacrifice a stand of principle would entail.
We are not only irresponsible but selfish,
our thoughts more often than not
concerned simply with our own satisfaction
and the pleasure of the moment.

We forget the needs of those around us,
we ignore the cry of the poor across the world,
and we ride roughshod over the claims of future generations
to their rightful stake in your creation.
We are part of a world in which the few have plenty
and the rest make do with crumbs from the table;
a world in which the well-being of the future
is sacrificed to the whims of the present;
and once more we have remained silent,
telling ourselves that there is nothing we can do
and so ducking the issue.

Gracious God,
we are reminded today
that thanksgiving must be more than simply words,
that it involves the stewardship of your gifts
and the generosity of our giving,
commitment both to you and to others.
Help us, as we celebrate another harvest,
to recognise that challenge and to act upon it. *Nick Fawcett*

124   Almighty and eternal God,
we rejoice this day in the greatness of your love,
the fullness of your provision.
We come together surrounded by the fruits of your creation,
the rich variety and plenty of another harvest.

Receive then our worship –
for your giving and sustaining of life,
for the constancy of the seasons,
for the regular pattern of day and night,
for the wonderful riches of our world.

Receive also our praise for the human labour
that is part of harvest –
the preparing and sowing,
the cultivating and growing,
the reaping and packaging,
the transporting and selling.

Eternal God,
we thank you that you allow us to work hand in hand
with you,
nurturing and gathering in the fruitfulness of your creation.
Help us to recognise the responsibility that involves,
and so to be faithful stewards of all you have given.
So may our lives as well as our words
offer to you our joyful thanksgiving and heartfelt worship.

Nick Fawcett

125   Loving God,
we bring you this day our thanksgiving
for everything you have given us.
We thank you for the infinite beauty of our world,
for the complexity of the universe,
for the wonder of creation that can never be exhausted.
We thank you for the constant miracle of day and night,
summer and winter,
springtime and harvest,
the regular cycle of life that we know and depend on.

We thank you for the rich resources of this planet,
and for all those who labour in different ways
to make them accessible to us.
We thank you for minds with which to understand,
enquire and learn,
for senses with which to see, hear, smell, taste and touch,
and for health to enjoy, savour and celebrate.

Forgive us that sometimes we lose our sense of
thankfulness,
becoming complacent and over-familiar
with the richness of creation.
Forgive us for taking your many gifts for granted,
forgetting them,
squandering them,
even abusing them.

Loving God,
give us a new sense of joy and gladness,
hearts that are truly thankful.
Help us to recognise again the awesome riches of creation,
and to rejoice in the blessings which you shower upon us.

Nick Fawcett

126 Living God,
creator of all that is, and has been, and shall be,
we thank you for this glad season and this special day.
We thank you for our world
with all its rich and wonderful variety,
for your gift of life
constantly being renewed by your loving hand,
for all that you have made to grow and flourish around us,
all that provides our food and clothing,
all the bountiful resources of this astonishing planet.

We thank you for those to whom we owe this harvest –
workers on farms and in agriculture,
sailors and fishermen
who risk their lives on the seas,
miners and engineers
who help supply the raw materials for industry,
scientists and technicians

who help develop better crops,
employees in shops and factories
who labour to satisfy our demands.

Living God,
help us to appreciate all so many do
to bring us the fruits of creation,
and teach us the part we must play
in ensuring future generations can enjoy it in turn.
Teach us to use your gifts wisely,
responsibly
effectively,
so that nothing may be needlessly wasted
or foolishly squandered.
Help us to remember those who do not share equally
in the rewards of harvest –
the poor,
the hungry,
the homeless,
the oppressed,
those overwhelmed by disaster,
and those whose crops have failed.
Save us, we pray, from selfish indulgence,
looking to our comforts and ignoring their needs.
Inspire us to share from our plenty
with all who cry out for help.

Living God,
you have provided beyond our needs,
enough for all in every place
to have enough and more than enough.
Forgive us that some still go hungry,
and forgive our part within that.
Stir our hearts so that we may challenge
the consciences of governments and nations,
until the time comes at last
when your gifts are shared and universally enjoyed.
You have blessed us in so much,
help us to respond,
in the name of Christ.   *Nick Fawcett*

127 Teach us, Lord,
that the skills and ingenuity you have given humankind
can either sustain your creation or destroy it.
Remind us that the fate of the planet is in our hands,
each of us having a part to play.
Help us faithfully to do our bit,
and grant that others may do the same. *Nick Fawcett*

128 Lord of all,
as we thank you for our harvest
we remember those who do not celebrate –
those whose harvest is poor or non-existent,
those with insufficient resources to tend their land,
those denied a just reward for their labours,
those whose harvest has been destroyed
in the chaos of war or by natural disaster.
Lord, you have blessed us richly:
teach us to remember others.

Help us, as we celebrate our plenty,
to remember those who have so much less –
the poor and needy of our world,
driven by famine, disaster or civil war
to the brink of starvation.
Help us to respond with love and concern,
offering whatever help we can.
Lord, you have blessed us richly:
teach us to remember others.

Lord of all,
speak to us at this harvest time,
so that our hearts may be stirred
and our consciences quickened.
Teach us to share our bounty with those who have nothing,
so that the time may one day come
when all have enough and none too much.
Lord, you have blessed us richly:
teach us to remember others,
in the name of Christ. *Nick Fawcett*

129 Creator God,
we pray for those to whom we owe our harvest,
all whose labour and dedication enables us
to share in the bounty of this world's resources.
We pray for farmers at this time of difficulty for so many –
a time of so much change and so many complex issues,
one crisis and controversy following upon another,
with a corresponding sense of mistrust and anxiety
among consumers.
Grant your help in overcoming adversity.

We pray for farmers in other lands –
denied the resources they need to cultivate their land,
overwhelmed by drought, flood or other catastrophe,
oppressed by exploitative regimes
or economic systems loaded against them –
both they and their people unable to enjoy
the due fruits of their labours.
Grant them hope, help and justice.

We pray for those who bring in the harvest of earth
and sea –
minerals, oil, gas, fish –
a harvest often involving danger to life and limb.
Grant them skill, courage and protection.

We pray for those who make possible the harvest
of technology –
scientists, technicians, computer programmers
and engineers –
their skills opening up new worlds and untold horizons,
capable of so much good yet so much evil.
Grant them wisdom, ingenuity and a due sense of
responsibility.

We pray for those who help to reap the harvest of minds –
teachers, students, researchers and scholars –
each striving to expand our knowledge and enlarge our
understanding.
Give them patience, dedication and integrity.

Creator God,
hear our prayer for all who make available
the innumerable and diverse riches of your creation.
Equip, inspire and guide them in their work,
so that they may steward your gifts wisely
to the good of all.
In the name of Jesus Christ our Saviour.   *Nick Fawcett*

130   May God
who clothes the flowers
and feeds the birds of the sky,
who leads the lambs to pasture
and the deer to water,
who multiplied loaves and fishes
and changed water into wine,
lead us,
feed us,
multiply us
and change us,
until we reflect
the glory of our Creator
through all eternity.   *Ray Simpson*

131   *Harvest Eucharist*
Provider God,
as autumn light ripens the grain,
ripen too our souls.
As brown leaves fall and sheaves are stored,
help us to fall into your ground
and store up deepening compassion.   *Ray Simpson*

132   As the grains of wheat
were scattered on a thousand fields
and now become one in this loaf,
so may we,
who are scattered in a thousand directions,
become one body in Christ.   *Ray Simpson*

Remembrance Day

133 Sovereign God,
we praise you today for the freedom we enjoy
as a nation and as individuals –
freedom of speech and expression,
freedom from war and oppression –
a freedom secured at such enormous human cost.
We praise you for those who made such freedom possible,
the countless thousands who sacrificed life and limb
in two World Wars
and in subsequent conflicts,
leaving homes and loved ones, often to return no more.

We praise you for all who have fought against tyranny,
hatred and evil,
prepared to sacrifice everything
rather than allow such forces to hold sway;
and we salute their courage shown in the face of danger,
their dedication to duty,
their determination to battle on against all odds.

We praise you for the peace we enjoy today –
a peace which we need to treasure constantly,
nurture carefully
and safeguard always,
recognising the price at which it was won.
We praise you for those today who fight
for international freedom and justice –
members of UN peacekeeping forces
in places of continuing tension,
striving to maintain democracy,
to keep rival factions apart,
to protect innocent civilians,
and to pave the way for a lasting end to hostilities.

Sovereign God,
we praise you today for the freedom we enjoy,
and we pray that the day will come
when there will be no more war,
when the nations of our world will live in harmony,
and when you will rule over all.

Until that time, help us to learn the lessons of the past,
to remember its sacrifices,
and to work as far as we are able for peace.   *Nick Fawcett*

134   Loving God,
we are reminded today of how easy it is to speak of peace,
and how difficult it is to pursue it;
how straightforward it sounds to talk of breaking down
barriers,
yet how demanding it is actually to live as peacemakers.
Yet we are reminded also that this is what you want from
us –
to live in such a way that we heal wounds
rather than create them,
that we unite rather than divide,
that we reconcile rather than separate.

We confess the things within us which make for conflict –
pride,
greed,
envy,
intolerance,
our nursing of petty grievances,
our unwillingness to forgive,
our preoccupation with self and our lack of time for
others –
so much that we are as guilty of as any other.

Rescue us from all that keeps us apart,
and put a new spirit within us –
a spirit of love and openness,
acceptance and understanding,
healing and reconciliation.
May the peace we pray for begin here and now in our hearts,
and so may we be instruments of your peace,
bringing healing to our broken world,
and harmony between nations.
In the name of Christ.   *Nick Fawcett*

135 Living God,
on this day we are called to remember the past –
all those who lost their lives in the course of war,
the horror they endured,
the determination they displayed
to defend the values we hold so dear today,
the sacrifices they made
so that we now might enjoy lasting peace.

Living God,
forgive us that, despite our words, all too easily we forget –
we fail to learn the lessons of the past,
we forget the debt we owe,
we take for granted the security we enjoy,
we do not work for the kind of world
so many gave their lives for.

Living God,
let there be peace in our world where now there is war,
and grant that the time will come
when nations will live together,
justly,
openly,
and harmoniously
in a common fellowship of humankind.
Lord, in your mercy,
hear our prayer
in the name of the one who came in peace,
Jesus Christ our Lord.   *Nick Fawcett*

136 Almighty God,
we thank you today for all those
who across the ages have been examples of courage,
all whose words and actions
have given inspiration to subsequent generations.
In glad thanksgiving,
we will remember them.

We thank you for those who have had the courage
to stand up for their convictions, come what may;
to fight against evil and injustice,
even at the cost of their own lives;

to live out their faith and share it with others
in the face of bitter opposition.
In glad thanksgiving,
we will remember them.

And especially this day we thank you
for those who displayed such courage
in all the horror of war –
those who fought so bravely,
who served so faithfully,
and who sacrificed so greatly
for the cause they believed in.
In glad thanksgiving,
we will remember them.

We give thanks for the freedom we enjoy
through their sacrifice,
we salute their courage,
we acknowledge again the debt we owe them,
and we remember, so that the lessons of the past
may not be forgotten or the sacrifices wasted.
In glad thanksgiving,
we will remember them.
Thanks be to God.   *Nick Fawcett*

137   Remind us, Lord,
      lest we forget,
      of the debt we owe –
      the life made possible
      through the death of others.
      Help us to cherish and nurture the things they died for –
      liberty,
      justice and peace –
      so that their sacrifice will not have been in vain.
                                                        Nick Fawcett

138   Lord of all,
      as we remember today the slaughter and sacrifice of war,
      the horror and heroism,
      fear and despair,
      pain and heartbreak,

help us to appreciate more fully the price paid
and the debt we owe to so many.
Reminded of the awfulness of conflict
teach us truly to appreciate the freedom we enjoy
and in a world still broken
may we strive always for peace,
working towards healing and harmony in all we do.

Nick Fawcett

139   Lord God,
in a world that's still divided,
marred by chasms of fear, hatred, envy
and injustice between so many,
help us to build bridges –
to do what we can,
where we can,
to construct links,
create dialogue
and promote partnership,
bringing together those previously kept apart.
Where barriers estrange and rifts alienate,
help each of us to be a peacemaker.   *Nick Fawcett*

140   Almighty God,
why don't you control this world you've made,
putting an end to its hatred, sorrow, pain and death?
Why don't you turn war to peace,
evil to good,
and darkness to light?
It's hard sometimes,
when we look at history with all its turmoil and conflict,
not to wonder why you seem to sit back
and allow it to happen.

But, of course, you can and do change things,
only not by force but by consent,
inviting our response rather than controlling our actions.
Move in the hearts of people everywhere,
challenging and transforming,
so that nations may seek peace and justice,
a world at one with itself and with you.   *Nick Fawcett*

141   Grant not just peace, Lord,
        but reconciliation in our world,
        an end to all that divides and destroys,
        so that those previously estranged may come together,
        shoulder to shoulder,
        heart to heart.
        Heal our wounds,
        and bring us harmony,
        in the name of Christ.   *Nick Fawcett*

142   Almighty God,
        we come this day to remember and learn –
        to remember the lessons of the past:
        the cost of war,
        the price of peace,
        the scope of human depravity,
        the extent of human self-sacrifice.
        Help us to learn those lessons –
        to live and work for peace,
        to fight only what is evil and corrupt,
        to serve and not to count the cost,
        to give our all in the cause of a better world.

        Almighty God,
        we come to remember all you have done –
        your creative acts,
        your mighty deeds throughout history,
        your dealings with your people,
        your gift of Christ,
        your love experienced daily in our lives.
        Remind us of all we owe,
        lest we forget.
        Forgive us that so often and so easily we do forget.
        We fail to remember your sovereign transforming power,
        to remember you in the good times as well as the bad,
        to see you in the fellowship of your Church,
        to count our many blessings,
        to recognise your hand at work
        in every moment of our lives.

Almighty God,
through all things you remember us –
help us to remember you!
We ask it in the name of Christ.   *Nick Fawcett*

*This prayer may be used following the traditional time of
silence and words of remembrance*

143 Loving God,
once more we have been reminded
of the terrible cost of war,
the suffering and sacrifice of so many,
the depths of inhumanity some have sunk to,
and the heights others have climbed
in the service of others.
Teach us to remember,
not just today but always.

We have heard again today words
which have been spoken so often over the years,
words which we ourselves have shared time and again:
'Lest we forget.'
Yet the tragedy is we do forget, all too easily –
this annual remembrance all too easily a token gesture,
observed sincerely and respectfully
but then over and done with for another year.
Teach us to remember,
not just today but always.

We forget how fortunate we are to live in freedom,
how lucky we are to enjoy peace.
We forget how some still suffer from the wounds of battle,
and others even now mourn their loved ones.
Teach us to remember,
not just today but always.

Loving God,
forgive us that, despite our words and best intentions,
we have so often forgotten the lessons of the past.
Speak to us through all we have heard and shared today,
so that we can truly say,
and truly mean,
'We will remember them.'   *Nick Fawcett*

144 Living God,
we are here to remember –
to remember again the awful cost of war,
to remember the millions
who gave their lives for the cause of freedom,
to remember the courage and heroism,
fear and pain, tragedy and grief of so many.
At the going down of the sun, and in the morning,
we will remember them.

Living God,
we are here to remember all of this, and much more
besides –
those who still mourn the loved ones they lost,
those whose lives even now are blighted by war,
those scarred in body, mind or spirit,
those for whom warfare has meant
life can never be the same again.
At the going down of the sun, and in the morning,
we will remember them.

And we remember also those who strive
to establish and maintain peace –
governments and world leaders,
United Nations' forces and diplomats,
pressure groups and ordinary people;
all who in different ways strive
to promote harmony between nations,
giving victims of war the opportunity
to live a normal life once more.
At the going down of the sun, and in the morning,
we will remember them.

Living God,
we remember today the cost of war,
and the price of peace.
Help us to go on remembering, tomorrow and every day,
and to do all in our power to work for your kingdom,
here on earth.
At the going down of the sun, and in the morning,
we will remember them,
in the name of Christ.

Nick Fawcett

145   Lord of all,
hear us now as we pray for the victims of war
and for peace in our world.
We pray for those across the world who bear the scars
of conflict –
the injured, maimed and mentally distressed,
those who have lost their limbs, their reason or their
loved ones
through the horrors of war.

We pray for those left homeless or as refugees,
those who have lost their livelihoods and security,
and those who still live in daily fear for their lives.
We pray for children who have been orphaned,
parents who mourn their children,
husbands and wives who have lost their partners –
countless families whose lives will never be the same again.

We pray for those in the armed forces,
charged with keeping the peace in countries across
the world –
their work involving months away from family and friends,
and often danger to themselves.
We pray for world leaders and rulers,
politicians and diplomats –
those whose decisions and negotiations
affect the lives of so many,
and in whose hands peace ultimately lies.

Lord of all,
give wisdom to all who work for peace,
so that a more secure future may be ensured for all.
Give courage to those who strive for justice,
so that the causes of conflict may be overcome.
Give strength to those who seek to break down barriers,
that divisions over race, colour, creed and culture may
be ended.
Grant that wherever war, or the threat of war,
continues to haunt lives,
a way of reconciliation may be found,
and harmony established between people and nations.
In the name of Christ.   *Nick Fawcett*

146 Immortal God,
as leaves fall to the ground
we recall the fallen in war.
In the barrenness of trees without leaf
may they and we turn to you.   *Ray Simpson*

147 To those who were snatched from Earth by violent death,
Holy Jesus, grant rest eternal.
To those whose sleep is stolen by the ravages of memory,
Holy Jesus, grant rest eternal.
We pray for an end to the injustices
that become breeding grounds of war.
We pray for the restoration of fellowship
and the building of integrity.   *Ray Simpson*

148 Creator God,
who brings one day to a close and a new day to dawn,
we remember those who gave their today
that we might have a tomorrow;
when the lights went out in two world wars
and in many lesser conflicts;
when millions died in foul trenches or mass genocide;
when six million died in gas chambers;
when many died from acts of terror or revenge.
We mourn for the goodness and wisdom
that died with them;
for the skill and wit that perished,
the learning, the laughter and the leadership that were lost.
The world has become a poorer place
and our hearts become cold
as we think of the splendour that might have been.
Echoes a Reform Jewish prayer   *Ray Simpson*

149 We remember the waste of life and wit and learning.
We remember the love that was never shared.
We remember the torture of body and mind.
We remember those who died
without understanding or valour.

We remember those who have no grave
to mark their sacrifice.
Still stands your Eternal Sacrifice.
Lord God of hosts, be with them yet. *Ray Simpson*

150 Saviour God, as we,
the communion of the living,
salute the communion of the dead,
heal the ancient wound that festers in humanity's heart.
Release compassion in places
where much blood has been shed.
Heal those
who can barely live with memories of injury or loss.
Salvage hope from the wrecks of time. *Ray Simpson*

151 Christ, linking us across the shores of treachery and time,
we give you thanks:
for the heroism of those who served in armed services
or on the home front
to provide relief, medical care or supplies;
for the patient suffering of the inhabitants
through the time of scarring;
for the dedication of those
who kept alight the torch of freedom
and sustained hope in others
for the reconstruction of communities
and the reconciliation of peoples
of different nationality and creed
following the years of destruction.
We pray for commitment to the unending struggle
against selfish ways and violation of human dignity.
We pray for that peace
which is the full blossoming of our life together.
Ray Simpson

Mothering Sunday

152 Gracious God,
as a mother loves her child so you love us.
For that great truth
we praise and thank you.
We owe our very lives to you.
You have watched over us from our birth,
tenderly nurturing us,
showering us with love.
When we have needed you, you have been there.
You have given us strength in times of need,
comfort in times of distress,
encouragement in times of despair,
guidance in times of uncertainty.
Whatever we have faced, you have been with us.

Gracious God,
we have not always appreciated your love,
all too often ignoring what you would teach us,
disobeying your instructions,
taking you for granted and wandering far from your side.
Yet through it all your love has remained constant.

Gracious God,
caring for us more than you care for yourself,
sacrificing your all for our sakes,
loving us with an unquenchable love,
you have called us all to be your children.
For that great truth
we praise and thank you,
in the name of Christ.

Nick Fawcett

153 Gracious God,
on this special day of thanksgiving
we catch a glimpse,
through a mother's love for her child,
of your love for us;
the care, dedication and devotion you show to all
your children

which makes you as much 'our Mother' as 'our Father'.
For the intensity of your love,
Lord, we praise you.

As a mother nurtures her children,
instructing,
feeding,
clothing,
guiding,
so you nurture us,
carefully leading us towards maturity.

As a mother tends her children,
comforting in times of distress,
reassuring in times of uncertainty,
encouraging in times of challenge,
nursing in times of sickness,
so you tend us,
always there to lift us up
and set us on our feet again when we fall.

As a mother protects her children,
watching over them day by day,
alert to danger,
keeping them from harm,
and ready if necessary to sacrifice herself for their sakes,
so you protect us,
your arms constantly encircling us,
your hand delivering us from evil.

Gracious God,
Mother and Father of us all,
we rejoice today in the wonder of your love
and the constancy of your care.
Gratefully we respond,
in joyful worship
and heartfelt thanksgiving.
For the intensity of your love,
Lord, we praise you.
In the name of Christ, your only Son.   *Nick Fawcett*

154 Forgive us, Lord,
for we take you for granted,
forgetting the way you hold us in your arms,
as a mother cradles her child;
the way you teach,
provide,
comfort and lead,
always there when we need you most.
Help us to respond,
not just today but every day,
in grateful and loving service.

Nick Fawcett

155 Gracious God,
we are reminded today
of how easily we take a mother's love for granted,
failing to express our thanks for the care we receive,
slow to demonstrate our appreciation
for the patient nurture given over so many years.

We are reminded equally of how easily we take your love
for granted,
failing to thank you for the blessings you shower upon us,
the care with which you daily surround us,
and the joy with which you fill our lives.
We have assumed that words do not need saying,
that our thankfulness can be taken as read.
We have believed love comes easily,
failing to recognise what it can sometimes cost.
We have imagined because no thanks is asked
that no thanks is necessary.

Gracious God,
help us to understand the joy we can bring
through saying thank you,
not just today but every day,
not just to our mothers but to everyone,
and not just to everyone but to you.
And help us, through the act of thanksgiving,
to recognise how much we have to be thankful for.

Nick Fawcett

156 Gracious God,
on this special day we thank you for mothers –
our own mothers and mothers everywhere.
We thank you for all they do, or once did,
all they give, or once gave,
all they mean, and will always mean.

Grant to all entrusted with the responsibility of
motherhood
your wisdom,
your guidance,
your support.
We thank you that you love us as a mother loves her child –
passionately, fiercely, devotedly, wholeheartedly –
and that, like a mother, you watch over us
every moment of every day,
seeking our welfare,
concerned about our progress,
equipping us for the journey of life.
You are always there when we need you,
ready to comfort, encourage and reassure,
slow to punish and swift to bless.

Gracious God,
we call you 'our Father',
but equally you are our Mother.
Help us to learn what that means,
and to rejoice in that truth.

Nick Fawcett

157 Loving God,
we thank you for mothers –
for all they mean or have meant to us,
for the love they have shown,
and the care they have given.
We thank you for the dedication of mothers –
the sacrifices they make,
the support they offer,
the comfort they bring,
and the guidance they provide.

We thank you for the qualities of mothers –
their patience,
kindness,
concern
and understanding.
We thank you for the role of mothers,
the part they play in our lives,
our homes,
our society
and our world.

We thank you for the joy of mothers –
the pleasure,
enrichment,
laughter and fulfilment,
which raising children brings.
We thank you for time spent with mothers –
the learning,
playing,
caring and sharing,
which are part of family life.

Loving God,
we thank you for this day of saying thank you,
this opportunity to say what we so often mean to say
but so rarely do.
For mothers and motherhood,
for children and families,
we bring you this day our grateful praise.   *Nick Fawcett*

158   Loving God,
       we thank you for this day –
       this day of remembering,
       rejoicing,
       and responding.
       We thank you for our homes and all we associate with
       them –
       the joy of family life,
       the debt we owe to our parents,
       and especially today the love of our mothers across the years.

We thank you for the much wider family of which we are
a part –
the family of humankind,
of this fellowship,
and the Church universal.
We thank you for the love you show us –
the same love a mother feels for her child,
the same patience and understanding,
the same concern and protectiveness.

Loving God,
grant your blessing upon all mothers and all families this day;
upon the family of humankind the world over,
upon the family of your Church, here and everywhere.
And grant your special care and support
to all those deprived of a mother's love,
and all those who have not yet come to know
your love for themselves.
Lord of all,
hear our prayer,
in the name of Christ.   *Nick Fawcett*

159 Caring and compassionate God,
speak to us today through the love shown by mothers
of your love for us and all:
the love that brought us into being,
that has nurtured us across the years,
that welcomes us here
and that will go on reaching out,
come what may,
for all eternity.

Help us, as we honour what motherhood means,
to honour you also,
recognising that you show the same devotion and more,
an unswerving commitment to your children's welfare;
and teach us, as part of your family,
to respond accordingly,
loving you in return,
expressing our gratitude,
and living as you have taught us,
through Jesus Christ our Lord   *Nick Fawcett*

160 Gracious God,
you know what it is to love your children –
to watch over them tenderly, anxiously,
proudly, and constantly.
You know what this means,
for you have called us your children,
and you care for each of us
as deeply as a mother cares for her child.

So now we pray for those
entrusted with the responsibility of motherhood –
all those who watch over their children in the same way,
with the same feelings and intensity.
Grant to each one your wisdom, guidance, and strength.

We pray especially for single mothers –
those faced with the challenge
of raising a child or children on their own,
with no one else to share the demands or joys of parenthood.
Give to each of them patience, devotion, and dedication.

We pray for those who have lost their mothers
or have never known them,
those orphaned as children or given up for adoption,
those whose mothers have died;
all for whom this day brings pain rather than pleasure.
Grant them your comfort, your support,
and the assurance of your love always with them.

We pray finally for those who are separated from their
children –
those whose children have moved far from home,
those who have suffered a miscarriage
or been through an abortion,
those who have endured the agony of a child's death.
Give to them your help, your solace, and hope for the
future.

Gracious God,
you understand what mothers face,
what they give,
what they feel.

Accept our thanks for them this day,
and grant them your special blessing.
Lord of love,
hear our prayer,
in the name of Christ.   *Nick Fawcett*

161   Gracious God,
on this Mothering Sunday we bring you our prayers
for all entrusted with the responsibility of motherhood.
We pray for mothers the world over,
recognising both the joys and demands they experience –
the privilege and pressures,
hopes and fears,
pleasure and pain that motherhood entails.
Equip them with the love, wisdom and strength they need.

We pray for single mothers,
bearing the responsibility of parenthood alone,
struggling sometimes to make ends meet,
and stigmatised by certain sections of society.
Grant them the emotional, physical and financial resources
they need.

We pray for mothers who have experienced heartbreak –
their children stillborn or seriously disabled,
injured, maimed or killed through accident or assault,
struck down by debilitating disease or terminal illness.
Comfort them in their sorrow.

We pray for those denied the joy of motherhood –
enduring the trauma of infertility,
prevented on health grounds from risking a pregnancy,
or unable to establish a relationship
into which children can be born.
Help them to come to terms with their pain.

We pray for those who foster or adopt children,
those who long to do so but who are denied the opportunity,
and those who for various reasons
have given up their children
and who are haunted by the image of what might have been.
Grant them your strength and support.

We pray finally for those who long to discover their
natural mothers,
those who have become estranged from them,
and those whose mothers have died –
all for whom Mothering Sunday brings pain rather
than pleasure,
hurt rather than happiness.
May your love enfold them always.

Gracious God,
we pray for mothers and children everywhere.
May your blessing be upon them,
your hand guide them,
and your love enrich them all.   *Nick Fawcett*

162   Lord God,
we thank you for our earthly opportunities for
mothering and being mothered,
we also remember
the mothering of you,
our parent God.   *Susan Sayers*

163   We pray to you, our loving parent God,
as children in one family.
We thank you, loving God,
for giving us one another to enjoy,
to laugh and cry with, to learn to live with.
May even our conflicts and arguments be used
in helping us to grow up in your love.   *Susan Sayers*

164   Thank you, loving God, for showing us the way to love
and giving us opportunities to give,
to take second place, to accept people as they are,
to forgive them when they annoy us,
and look for their needs before our own.   *Susan Sayers*

165   Thank you, loving God, for the world we live in,
for the colours and shapes, the sounds and textures in it.
Thank you for giving us minds and emotions
and help us to reverence the whole of creation. *Susan Sayers*

166 Thank you, loving God, for comfort and sympathy,
reassurance and practical caring when we are ill or sad.
Make us all more aware of the needs of those around us
and let our loving show in action.   *Susan Sayers*

167 Thank you, loving God,
for your promise to be with us always,
and not just until we die.
We remember with affection
our parents who loved us into existence.
Gather us up into your loving arms
and comfort us even when our
memories remind us of loss and heartache.   *Susan Sayers*

168 Thank you, loving God,
for giving us
space and support,
guidance and forgiveness,
challenge and reassurance.   *Susan Sayers*

169 We gather together
in the presence of you, our parent God.
You provide comfort
in all our troubles and sufferings.
We are all your children:
help us grow in love.   *Susan Sayers*

170 We thank you for the example of those
whose faith shines out through love in their lives.
                                                 Susan Sayers

171 Loving Father,
we give you thanks
for the comfort you provide
in all our troubles,
and for the richness
of all our relationships.   *Susan Sayers*

172 Lord, into our lives and relationships
pour the insight and discernment we need.
May we learn to love you more
as we learn to live and work in harmony,
focused on you and not on our divisions.
Pour the reality and wholesome truth we need,
that we may learn mutual trust
and support one another in love. *Susan Sayers*

173 Lord, into the laughter and tears of family life
pour the freshness of your living presence,
as we work at our relationships
and deepen our love for one another. *Susan Sayers*

Father's Day

174 Loving God,
we come on this Father's Day,
reminded that you are the Father of us all.
You have been with us from our birth,
guiding, nurturing, and sustaining us.
Father God,
we praise you.

You have taught us and brought us to maturity,
always concerned for our welfare,
constantly seeking the best for us.
Father God,
we praise you.

Whenever we have needed you, you have been there,
willing to listen and advise,
yet giving us freedom to make our own choices
and find our own way.
Father God,
we praise you.

You have called us to be your family,
a people united through your Son, Jesus Christ,
and through him you have revealed your love,
a love that reaches out to us day by day
despite our failure to love you in return.

Father God,
we praise you.

Teach us to live as your children –
to hear your voice,
obey your instruction,
and respond to your goodness.
Father God,
we praise you.

Teach us to bear your name with pride,
to share with others,
through word and deed,
the joy you have given us.
Father God,
we praise you.

And finally receive our thanks
for the fathers you have given us,
all they have meant to us,
all they have given,
and all they have done in so many ways.
Father God,
we praise you,
in the name of Christ.

Nick Fawcett

175 Sovereign God,
Creator of the heavens and the earth,
Ruler over space and time,
we praise you that we can respond to you as a Father;
that we can approach you,
not in a spirit of subservience or fear,
but as your children,
assured of your love and secure in your purpose.

We praise you that you care for us
as much as any father cares for his child
and far more besides –
your hand always there to guide and discipline,
to provide and protect,
to comfort and encourage,
to nurture and cherish.

We praise you that your love is inexhaustible –
that, however often we fail you,
however many times we may stray from your side,
you seek us out,
striving to restore the relationship we have broken,
always ready to forgive and forget.

We praise you that we are made in your image,
capable of understanding good and evil,
able to appreciate treasure in heaven
as well as the many riches of this world,
and able also to respond to your love in Christ
and so inherit your kingdom.

Sovereign God,
we come to you on this Father's Day,
giving thanks for everything that fathers mean to us,
but rejoicing above all in your fatherly care for all.
With grateful hearts, we bring you praise,
and commit ourselves again to your service.   *Nick Fawcett*

176   Loving God,
we come together on this Father's Day,
reminded not just of our earthly fathers but of you.
You tell us that all who believe in you
shall be called your children,
and you invite us to address you quite simply as 'our Father'.
For the wonder of your love,
we praise you.

We praise you that, despite all our weakness and disobedience,
you view us not as subjects,
or as servants,
but as children.
And we rejoice that you want us to see you
not as some deity remote in splendour,
nor as a jealous God demanding our homage,
but as a father, watching over us
with infinite care and tenderness.
For the wonder of your love,
we praise you and worship your holy name.   *Nick Fawcett*

177 Gracious God,
we call you 'our Father',
but we rarely live as your children ought to live.
We are stubborn, wilful and disobedient,
repeatedly rejecting your guidance,
time and again betraying your love.
Father,
forgive us.

We speak of being called into your family,
but we are often a family divided,
allowing petty disputes,
anger, bitterness, envy and resentment,
to come between us.
Father,
forgive us.

We claim to be made in your image,
but there is very little of you to be seen in us.
We find it hard to love,
difficult to forgive
and almost impossible to let go of self.
Father,
forgive us.

We tell ourselves that our relationship with you is a
close one,
that through Christ we can call you 'Abba, Father',
but the truth is that we stray far from your side, day
after day,
oblivious to your presence
and unconcerned about the gulf this creates between us.
Father,
forgive us.

Gracious God,
forgive us everything that holds us back from knowing you,
that prevents us enjoying the special relationship
you long to share with us.
Help us to respond joyfully and spontaneously to your love,
and, in childlike trust,
to receive the blessings you so long to give us.

Come to us now,
and draw us closer to yourself.
Through Jesus Christ our Lord.   *Nick Fawcett*

178   Gracious God,
you are the Creator of the ends of the earth,
and yet you call us your children.
You are greater than we can ever begin to imagine,
and yet you invite us to call you 'our Father'.
Always you have loved us:
forgive our feeble response.

You do not keep us at arm's length,
remote in your holiness,
but you reach out your hands in love,
wanting us to relate to you, one to one.
Always you have loved us:
forgive our feeble response.

Gracious God,
forgive us that we call you 'our Father',
but fail to live as your children.
We do not trust you as we should,
preferring instead to follow our own inclinations.
We are reluctant to accept your will,
repeatedly disobeying your instructions.
We are slow to seek your guidance,
but swift to forget you and wander from your side.
We all too rarely thank you for what we have,
but all too often complain
when we do not receive what we ask for.
Always you have loved us:
forgive our feeble response.

Gracious God,
we have returned your love by acting like spoilt children,
yet still you have kept faith.
Accept our thanks that, despite our wilfulness,
you refuse to give up on us,
working instead to draw us closer.

You are always there for us,
waiting to welcome us back
and set us on our feet again.
Always you have loved us:
forgive our feeble response.

Gracious God, our Father,
we praise and thank you for your undeserved goodness,
and we resolve today to live more faithfully as your children.
Always you have loved us:
forgive our feeble response.
In the name of Jesus Christ, your Son, our Lord.

Nick Fawcett

179   Gracious God,
we thank you today for fathers and for all that they do,
their role sometimes taken for granted
and yet meaning so much.
We thank you for our own fathers –
for all they have meant to us,
everything they have contributed to our lives,
and we acknowledge, with gratitude,
the support they have offered;
the care they have shown,
the instruction they have given,
and the love they have shared.

We thank you for the privilege of fatherhood –
the wonder of sharing in the creation of a new life,
the thrill of seeing a child mature into adulthood,
the awe-inspiring responsibility of nurturing, guiding,
enabling and encouraging,
and the sheer joy of giving and receiving love,
building a relationship that will endure for a lifetime and
beyond.

Gracious God,
we thank you for fathers
and, above all, we thank you for your fatherhood,
your creation of all,
your constant nurture,

your unfailing love which delights to call us your children
and which is always looking to draw us more deeply
into the family of your people. *Nick Fawcett*

180   Help us, Lord,
to show our love for you,
not through sophisticated language or polished prayers,
but through true commitment,
responding with childlike trust, gratitude and affection
to your fatherly care.
Teach us to open our hearts to you,
as you have so freely done to us. *Nick Fawcett*

181   Gracious God,
on this day for remembering, acknowledging
and celebrating fathers,
help us to remember that you call us your children
and that you ask us in turn to call you 'our Father'.

Teach us what that means:
that you care about our welfare;
that you provide for our needs and protect us from danger;
that you delight to bless and cherish;
that you strive to equip us for life,
to teach, guide, support and enable.

Help us, then, as we honour the place of fathers in our lives,
or commit ourselves more fully to faithful parenthood,
also to honour you,
growing and living obediently as your children,
so that we might attain maturity in Christ
and inherit the fullness of life you offer through him.
In his name we pray. *Nick Fawcett*

182   Gracious God,
you know the joy of fatherhood and also the pain,
for you witnessed the life and death of your Son,
and you see each day the triumphs and tragedies of us,
your children.
Lord God our Father,
reach out in love.

You experienced the delight of being a father –
as you watched Jesus grow and mature into adulthood,
as you saw him baptised in the Jordan,
as day by day he responded to your guidance,
faithful to the very last –
a beloved son with whom you were well pleased.
Yet also you experienced agony –
in the horror of the Cross,
the pain, the humiliation,
and the sorrow he endured for our sakes.
Lord God our Father,
reach out in love.

In each of us you find pleasure –
when we pursue what is good,
when we honour your commandments,
when we seek your will and respond to your guidance.
But we cause you also so much pain –
through our weakness,
our repeated disobedience,
our deafness to your call and our rejection of your love.
Lord God our Father,
reach out in love.

Gracious God,
you know the joy and the pain of fatherhood,
and so now we pray for fathers everywhere.
Help them to appreciate both the privilege
and the responsibility they bear,
and teach them to give freely of themselves
so that they may discover the happiness,
the fulfilment,
and the inexpressible rewards that fatherhood brings.
Lord God our Father,
reach out in love.

Give them wisdom, patience, and dedication,
and grant them strength to persevere
when children bring tears as well as laughter,
anxiety as well as hope,
pain as well as pleasure.

Lord God our Father,
reach out in love.

Reach out, we pray, to all fathers in such circumstances –
those who question their ability to cope,
or who fear they have failed;
those striving to offer support,
or who feel they have nothing left to give.
Lord God our Father,
reach out in love.

And finally hear our prayer for children
who on this Father's Day feel pain instead of joy –
those whose fathers have died,
those orphaned as children,
those who have been mistreated, rejected, abused,
and those from broken homes
who barely see or know their fathers.
Lord God our Father,
reach out in love,
through Jesus Christ our Lord.

Nick Fawcett

183 Father God,
we pray today for those entrusted with the responsibility
of fatherhood,
all who have the duty and privilege of raising children,
fashioning their lives,
offering a stable and loving environment in which they
can grow,
leading them along the exciting yet demanding path
to adulthood.
Grant them love, insight and devotion.

We pray for fathers whose marriage
or relationship with their partner has broken down;
separated from their children or seeing them only occasionally,
many having responsibilities for another family,
and we pray also for those
who will fill the role of stepfather.
Grant them commitment, dedication and sensitivity.

We pray for fathers with no sense of responsibility,
failing to make time for their children,
careless in offering support and guidance,
casual in providing discipline,
essentially washing their hands of their role as parents.
Grant them forgiveness, understanding
and the opportunity to make amends.

We pray for children of broken homes,
deprived of a father figure
or knowing first one, then another,
rarely able to establish a meaningful and lasting
relationship.
Grant them stability, support
and the knowledge that they are still loved.

We pray for children abused by their fathers,
emotionally scarred for life,
struggling to come to terms with their experience,
haunted by an image of fear rather than love.
Grant them healing, peace and courage to face the future.

Finally, we pray for those who have lost their fathers,
whether as children or as adults,
for some their father little more than a name,
for others, a heart-wrenching memory,
but each carrying a sense of loss.
Grant your strength, your comfort and your hope.

Father God,
we lift before you today fathers and their children.
Enfold them in your love,
and surround them with your fatherly care,
today and every day.
Through your Son, Jesus Christ our Lord.   *Nick Fawcett*

184   Loving Father,
          teach us not simply to say 'Our Father',
          but to mean it –
          to recognise that you love us as deeply,
          as dependably,

and as devotedly as any human father,
and infinitely more besides.
For the wonder of your love,
we praise you.

Teach us that we matter to you,
that you are concerned for our welfare,
that you delight to bless us,
that we need only to ask and you are there.
For the wonder of your love,
we praise you.

Teach us that it is because you care so much
that you instruct us,
discipline us,
and correct us.
For the wonder of your love,
we praise you.

Teach us that, however far we stray from you,
however much we may reject your love
or ignore your guidance,
still you go on reaching out,
longing to draw us close once more.
For the wonder of your love,
we praise you.

Loving God,
you are 'Our Father' and we praise you.
Teach us to be your children,
in the name of Christ.

Nick Fawcett

Adult Baptism/Confirmation

185 God of majesty,
you are the beginning and the end of all,
higher than our highest thoughts,
greater than we can ever begin to imagine,
defying expression in human terms.
There is nothing you are unable to do,
no one you are unable to change –

always you are at work within us,
reaching out to transform our lives.
Receive our praise,
in the name of Christ.

God of love,
we praise you for all you have done for us –
the good things we have received from your hands,
the guidance you have so faithfully given.
Though you are sovereign and wholly other,
yet you care for us all,
constantly striving to draw us closer,
longing to bless us with life in all its fullness.
Receive our praise,
in the name of Christ.

God of grace,
we praise you for your coming in Jesus Christ –
for speaking so powerfully of your love
through his birth and ministry,
his death and resurrection,
his ascension and exaltation.
We praise you for his continuing presence with us now
through his Holy Spirit,
nurturing our faith,
calling us to service and filling us with joy.
Receive our praise,
in the name of Christ.

God of mercy,
we praise you for the forgiveness you offer us
despite our failure to live as your people.
Though we repeatedly disobey you,
often ignore you,
and daily forget you,
still you continue to reach out,
calling us back and renewing us through your grace.
Receive our praise,
in the name of Christ.

God of life,
we thank you for accepting us as we are,
with all our faults and weaknesses,
and we thank you today
that you have called AB to faith in you,
leading him/her to this moment
through which he/she will publicly testify
to all that you mean in his/her life.
We thank you that as you welcome him/her,
so also you long to welcome each of us.
Receive our praise,
in the name of Christ.

Loving God,
meet with us now in this time of worship.
Help us to sense your nearness and hear your voice,
responding freely and gladly in faith,
not holding back or putting off,
but accepting your love
and rejoicing in all you have done for us.
Receive our praise,
in the name of Christ.

Nick Fawcett

186 Sovereign God,
we praise you for all the ways you work in our lives –
the fact that you love us before we ever know it,
call us before we realise you are able to use us,
and guide us before we even begin to respond.

We praise you that you call us,
not because we deserve it,
nor because we are in any way specially qualified to
serve you,
but solely by your grace,
reaching out in love day after day
until you have drawn us to yourself.

We praise you that you can use every one of us –
that we are all special in your sight,
able to receive the gifts of your Spirit
and contribute to the work of your kingdom.

We praise you that you have led AB to this point of decision,
this moment when he/she wants to respond to your love
and, of his / her own free will,
commit himself /herself to the service of Christ
and to his work within this church.

We praise you for everything that has led up to this
moment –
the reflection,
sharing,
friendship
and nurture
that have brought A to identify himself /herself
with this fellowship
and to confess Jesus Christ as his /her Lord and Saviour.

Sovereign God,
we praise you for A,
for everything he/she means to us,
for everything he/she means to you,
for everything we mean to each other.

Unite us in faith,
and bind us together in love,
so that the promises made now
may be honoured in the days ahead,
to the glory of your name.   *Nick Fawcett*

187   Gracious God,
if we say we have no sin, we deceive ourselves,
and the truth is not in us.
If we confess our sins,
you, who are faithful and just,
will forgive our sins
and cleanse us from all unrighteousness.
We thank you for that promise,
and we come now in faith,
acknowledging our sinfulness,
and seeking your pardon.

We may possibly deceive ourselves,
but we know we can never deceive you,
for you see us as we really are,
with all our faults and weaknesses,
our unworthy actions and ugly thoughts;
and so we come with shame,
acknowledging our dependence on your grace,
and seeking your pardon.

We have no claim on your goodness,
for, despite our best intentions,
our promises of commitment and pledges of loyalty,
we let you down time and again,
our words saying one thing,
our lives another;
and so we come with sorrow,
acknowledging our need of help,
and seeking your pardon.

We want to serve you,
we mean to follow the way of Christ,
but our hearts are fickle and our faith is flawed,
the spirit willing but the flesh weak;
and so we come in humility,
acknowledging our faithlessness,
and seeking your pardon.

Gracious God,
we thank you that you are a God slow to anger
and abounding in steadfast love,
a God who is swift to pardon
and delighting to forgive.

We praise you that you treat us
not according to our deserts
but according to your grace,
always ready to put the past behind us
and to help us to start again.

You invite us to wash and be clean,
to confess our sins and to receive your forgiveness;
and so we come now with joy,

acknowledging your grace
and assured of your pardon!
Through Jesus Christ our Lord.   *Nick Fawcett*

188   Loving God,
we thank you that you have brought AB to this point
of publicly declaring his/her faith in you.
We thank you for the joy and fulfilment
he/she has found in Christ,
discovering in him the way, the truth
and the life for themselves.
We praise you for all the ways you have guided,
nurtured and spoken to A;
for all the strength you have given, love you have shown,
and help you have offered.

Loving God,
we thank you for A,
and all this moment means to him/her.
And we thank you that you invite each of us in turn
to make our own individual response.
You call us, as you have called A,
not through any goodness on our part,
nor because we have all the answers and no questions,
but because you love us
and are ready to accept us as we are.

Loving God,
speak to us through this service,
so that we may hear your voice
and respond to your challenge.   *Nick Fawcett*

189   Lord Jesus Christ,
as we share today in this service of commitment –
this symbol of new beginnings
and celebration of your great mercy and love –
call us all to deeper faith,
greater trust,
stronger commitment
and truer devotion.

Remind us of the fresh start you have won for us,
the fulfilment you offer
and the blessings you long to impart,
and through sharing each day in your death and resurrection,
putting off the old and rising to the new,
may we know, honour, love and serve you more faithfully,
to the glory of your name.   *Nick Fawcett*

190   May the word of God guide your footsteps,
the power of God equip you for service,
the grace of God constantly renew you
and the love of God surround you always.

May your vision be clear,
your commitment strong,
and your faith constant.
May peace flood your soul
and light shine from your heart.

May Christ be your constant companion
on the path of discipleship,
until your journey is over
and you meet with God face to face,
secure in the joy of his everlasting kingdom.
The Lord bless and keep you,
now and for evermore.   *Nick Fawcett*

191   Living God,
we thank you for your call,
your gracious invitation to respond to your love
that goes on reaching out to us
until we have turned to you
and accepted the gift of new life you so long to give us.

We thank you for the way A has responded to that call,
publicly committing his/her life today to the service of Christ,
and we pray now for everything the future holds for him/her.
Grant your guidance, strength and inspiration,
keep his/her faith strong
and his/her love for you burning bright,
and may your blessing enrich his/her life.

We pray for all those who have committed their lives to you,
declaring Jesus Christ as their Lord and Saviour.
Equip them for service,
unite them in love,
empower them through your Spirit,
and bless them with peace.

We pray for those who resist your call,
afraid of what commitment might entail.
Conquer their doubts,
overcome their hesitation,
and may they discover the blessing they have been missing.

We pray for those who are unmoved by your call,
untouched by the message of the gospel.
Speak your word,
stir their hearts,
and touch their lives with your blessing.

We pray for those who have responded to your call
and then gone back,
the faith they once professed grown cold.
Rekindle the flame,
restore their vision
and may your blessing thrill them once more.

Living God,
may your word reach out with power,
creating, sustaining and renewing faith.
May your call touch our lives, today and always,
and may we respond with heartfelt devotion
and faithful service,
to the glory of your name.
Through Jesus Christ our Lord.   *Nick Fawcett*

192   In the days of Noah,
the dove brought an olive branch,
and news of peace from God.
May we who have been baptised
know the peace that the Holy Spirit brings.
                                    Gerald O'Mahony

193 We remember that by adoption
we are all God's beloved sons and daughters.
We too have a message
to give to a listening world,
a message of love and forgiveness.
May we not stay silent, dear Lord.   *Gerald O'Mahony*

194 We pray for those preparing for baptism,
and for the children and others not long since baptised.
May they realise the treasure
that has been given to them,
and never lose faith in your love, O God.   *Gerald O'Mahony*

195 Quietly we pray to know, deep in our hearts,
God's personal love for each one of us . . .

(Silent prayer)

Heavenly Father,
as your children we are well loved by you.
May we repay you by lives of faithful service,
through Christ our Lord.   *Gerald O'Mahony*

196 The message of Jesus means
we are all children of God,
and therefore sisters and brothers to one another.
Everyone I meet
is as precious to God as I am.
We pray to treat one another with respect,
with love and fairness,
and with compassion, as God loves us.   *Gerald O'Mahony*

197 At the baptism of Jesus,
the heavens were split open:
no barrier between heaven and earth.
May we learn to see you, our God,
through the eyes of Jesus your Son.   *Gerald O'Mahony*

198   Jesus is the beloved Son,
         yet he calls us his sisters and brothers.
         May God give us grateful hearts:
         God loves us, not because we are good children,
         but because we are his children.   *Gerald O'Mahony*

199   Jesus, you do not break the crushed reed,
         nor put out the wavering flame.
         Lord Jesus, bless those preparing for baptism this year.
         May they be aware that they are walking
         where you have walked before them,
         and that you will be their Shepherd.   *Gerald O'Mahony*

200   The prophet Hosea describes
         how God loved Israel
         as a father loves his little child.
         We thank Jesus who risked his life
         to tell us that God loves each one of us
         just like that.   *Gerald O'Mahony*

201   In our baptism,
         we are one with Jesus in his baptism:
         the Spirit comes like a dove with an olive branch,
         and the Father invites each one of us to call him
         Abba!, 'My Father!'   *Gerald O'Mahony*

202   Heavenly Father, we cannot thank you enough
         for adopting us as your first-generation children
         and part of your immediate family,
         through your own Son Jesus Christ,
         who lives and reigns with you for ever.   *Gerald O'Mahony*

203   Father, without your Spirit
         our hearts would be cold
         and our lives would be feeble and failing.
         Give us again, we pray, the gift of your Spirit,
         through Jesus Christ our risen Lord.   *Gerald O'Mahony*

204 In our baptism
we are each given our own place
at God's family table
as one of his children.
May we be ever grateful.   *Gerald O'Mahony*

205 In this new world as God's children,
we are free to work hard
for all the causes dear to your heart, Father God,
knowing we are allowed to make mistakes
without losing your love.   *Gerald O'Mahony*

206 Jesus, in your baptism
there was no barrier between you and the Father;
in your death you tore down the veil
between us and your Father.
How can we thank you enough
for opening up for us
the way home to God!   *Gerald O'Mahony*

207 Jesus, you were the first of us
to be caught in the net of God's love;
then you went about to catch the rest of us,
like a fisher casting his net.
We are blessed to have been 'caught' by you.
     Gerald O'Mahony

208 Jesus speaks of 'the children's food'.
Our Holy Communion is just that:
through baptism we have
each our own place at God's table,
and we are given the bread of the children.
Thanks be to God!   *Gerald O'Mahony*

209 God, you are here with us.
You know each of us completely
And love us completely.
Have mercy on us and send your Holy Spirit
to be with us all tonight and for ever.   *Susan Sayers*

210 Jesus, we believe that you are the son of God.
We believe that you entered our world as a human baby
and showed us, in the language of a human life,
exactly what God is like.
Your love for us is amazing.
You were even willing to give up your life and die on a cross
for us so that we could be set free to live to the full –
the way God created us to be.
Thank you, Jesus, for loving and accepting us as we are.
We want to invite you into our lives so that we live in you
and you in us.
We want to get to know you much better,
and grow more like you each day that we live. *Susan Sayers*

211 As we embark on our lifelong journey as followers of you,
Lord Jesus,
make us ready to affirm our faith in you with our own
mouths and hearts,
undertaken in the company of the community of
the Church,
in the confirmed strength and power
of the true and living God. *Susan Sayers*

212 We enter into God's family,
joining those newly baptised, recently confirmed
and all Christians through the ages,
for a deeper commitment to supporting one another
as we grow in faith. *Susan Sayers*

213 We pray in thankfulness
for those who introduced us to Jesus
and who help us along our spiritual journey.
We pray for one another in this church
and for all Christians, young and old,
throughout the world. *Susan Sayers*

214 Into the life of the Father I immerse you,
that he may protect you from harm,
bring you peace and calm.

Into the boundless life of your Maker I immerse you.
Into the life of the Son I immerse you,
that he may save you from hell,
keep you washed and well.
Into the sinless life of your Saviour I immerse you.
Into the life of the Spirit I immerse you,
that he may light up your night,
give you power to do right.
Into the endless life of your Soul Friend I immerse you.
Into the life of the Three I immerse you,
that they may fill you with love,
lift you to heaven above.
Into the selfless love of the Trinity I immerse you.

Ray Simpson

Infant Baptism

215 Sovereign God,
giver of life,
creator of all that is and has been,
sustainer of the universe,
we praise you.

Living God,
giver of joy,
of the blessings we receive each day
and of the love we share together,
we praise you.

Gracious God,
giver of mercy,
always forgiving,
constantly bringing renewal and restoration,
we praise you.

Faithful God,
giver of guidance,
for ever by our side,
instructing,
leading,

challenging,
equipping,
we praise you.

Generous God,
giver of all our needs,
providing,
nurturing,
nourishing,
fulfilling,
we praise you.

Creator God,
we come this day,
rejoicing in the new life you have given,
filled with joy,
trusting in your mercy,
and assured of your gracious guidance.

We come in celebration
to give thanks
and to commit ourselves and this child to you,
as, together, we praise you.
Through Jesus Christ our Lord.   *Nick Fawcett*

216 Living God,
Father of all,
we come today thanking you for the gift of this child,
with all the joy yet demands,
expectations yet responsibilities,
surrounding him/her.
We come also thanking you for the gift of eternal life,
new birth in Christ,
recognising equally the blessing yet challenge,
reward yet cost,
that this involves too.
Receive today the commitment that will be expressed
and vows made,
and, by your grace, lead each of us to discover in life now
the joy of life in all its fullness –
your gracious gift through Jesus Christ our Lord.
                                                  Nick Fawcett

217 Loving God,
we thank you for the gift of life and for the miracle of birth,
the wonder of a newborn child,
fashioned by your hand,
lovingly created,
and bringing such joy to so many.

We thank you for the life of AB,
for all that stretches before him/her –
the possibilities, joys and discoveries you hold in store,
the enrichment he/she will bring through his/her presence,
and the times we will share with him/her
over the years to come.

We thank you for the love that surrounds A –
the care of his/her parents,
the support of family and friends,
the prayers of this fellowship,
and your own everlasting arms.

We thank you for the happiness we share this day –
the joy A's birth has brought,
the hope it has kindled,
and the thanksgiving it has evoked.

We thank you for your gift of eternal life –
a life which begins here and now,
bringing peace, love and fulfilment,
yet which promises greater joys to come.

Loving God,
this is a day of thanksgiving, celebration and dedication,
a day to honour you
and to acknowledge your goodness.
Gladly we consecrate A to you
and joyfully we commit ourselves in the same faith.
Through Jesus Christ our Lord.   *Nick Fawcett*

218 AB,
the Lord watch over you, this and every day,
the Lord guide your footsteps and keep you from evil,
the Lord grant you health and strength, joy and fulfilment,
your whole life long.

The Lord be a blessing to you,
leading you in the way of peace, wisdom, love and humility,
so that you in turn may be a blessing to others.
The Lord fill you with light
and enfold you in love,
now and for evermore.
Through Jesus Christ our Lord.   *Nick Fawcett*

219   Creator God,
we worship you today for the gift of a new life.
We come with joy in our hearts,
to thank you for this child,
to praise you for all his/her birth means to us,
and all it means to you.
We thank you for the love that has brought A into being,
the care that surrounds him/her,
the excitement his/her arrival has brought,
and the happiness that he/she has given
to those around him/her.

Grant your blessing upon A.
Watch over him/her.
Guide his/her footsteps.
Protect him/her from danger.
Bless him/her with health.
Fill him/her with joy.
And in the fullness of your time
may he/she come to know your love,
and respond to you in faith,
discovering the joy and peace
that you alone can offer.

Creator God,
we pray also for C and D,
whom you have entrusted
with the responsibilities of parenthood –
give them wisdom,
patience,
devotion,
and dedication.

May A enrich their lives in immeasurable ways,
and may they in turn offer A the security
of a loving, caring home in which to grow.
Help them, through their words and actions,
to sow the seeds of your love in A's heart,
and then to give him/her space
to make his/her response in his/her own time and own way.

Creator God,
we thank you for this day,
this child,
and this family.
And we thank you for your love which surrounds us all,
this day and always.
Lord of life,
hear our prayer,
in the name of Christ.

Nick Fawcett

220   Gracious God,
we pray for AB in whatever the future may hold for him/her.
May your hand be there to lead,
and your love be there to bless.

Grant help to A in times of learning,
so that he/she may grow in wisdom and understanding,
in knowledge, skill and ability,
and in experience and character,
equipped to make the most of life's possibilities.
May your hand be there to lead,
and your love be there to bless.

Grant A your strength in times of testing –
the ability to overcome difficulties,
withstand trials,
and conquer temptation,
staying true to his/her convictions
and emerging stronger out of adversity.
May your hand be there to lead,
and your love be there to bless.

Grant your guidance in times of uncertainty –
discernment as to the right way forward,
patience in coming to a decision,
and confidence that a door will open,
your will ultimately becoming apparent.
May your hand be there to lead,
and your love be there to bless.

Grant your peace in times of turmoil –
the knowledge that, whatever may happen, you are there,
nothing ever able to separate us from your love,
and so may A be able
to meet changing circumstances of life with equanimity,
assured of your ultimate purpose.
May your hand be there to lead,
and your love be there to bless.

Grant your blessing in times of opportunity,
so that A may discover lasting love,
enduring joy,
and fulfilment in work, faith and life.
May your hand be there to lead,
and your love be there to bless.

Gracious God,
we ask you to put your hand upon A,
to watch over him/her,
to direct his/her footsteps
and to make known your love,
so that he/she may respond freely to you
in his/her own time and way.
May your hand be there to lead,
and your love be there to bless.
In the name of Christ we ask it.   *Nick Fawcett*

221   Gracious God,
        we thank you for your gift of children,
        for the joy, the laughter,
        and the fun they bring in so many ways.
        We thank you for their innate zest for life –
        the interest, excitement and fascination they find
        in so much we count ordinary.

We thank you for their special qualities –
their innocence, trust, enthusiasm, energy,
and sheer hunger to learn.
We lift them now to you:
open your heart to all.

We pray for this child presented to you this day,
and for children everywhere,
so precious to us,
so precious to you.
Watch over them,
protect them, guide them and bless them.

And hear also our prayer for those who are childless,
or who long to conceive another child.
Reach out to them in their pain, their frustration,
their disappointment, their anger.
Help them not to lose hope until all hope is past,
and if that time finally comes
give them the comfort you alone can bring,
and courage to channel their love to those around them.

Finally we pray for disadvantaged children –
those who are disabled, abused, orphaned,
undernourished, unloved, unwanted –
so many denied the start in life they deserve
and the care they need.

Loving God,
in Christ you welcomed little children,
demonstrating their importance to you,
their special place in your heart.
Prosper the work of all who care for children today –
all who strive to give them a better life,
a brighter future,
a safer world in which to grow.
Use them, and us, to make real your care for all.

Nick Fawcett

222   Gracious God,
        you have brought this child into being –
        go with him/her now in their journey of life.

May he/she know joy,
health,
and peace.
May he/she grow in love,
wisdom,
and faith.
Direct his/her steps,
keep him/her from evil,
and help him/her to live life in all its fullness,
this day and always.
In the name of Christ.   *Nick Fawcett*

*Three drops of warm water are poured on the baby's forehead,
one during each of the first three sentences*

223 A little drop of your Creator
on your forehead, precious one. Amen.
A little drop of your Saviour
on your forehead, precious one. Amen.
A little drop of your Guardian Spirit
on your forehead, precious one. Amen.
The little drop of the Three
to shield you from harm
to fill you with their virtue.   *Ray Simpson*

224 God our Creator,
in giving us this child you have shown us your love.
We thank you from our hearts for the joy of this child,
for the wonder of this life,
for a safe delivery
and for the privilege of being parents.   *Ray Simpson*

225 Circle her/him, Lord, keep peace within.
Circle her/him, Lord, keep love within.
Circle her/him, Lord, keep trust within.
Circle her/him, Lord, keep truth within.
Circle her/him, Lord, keep good within.   *Ray Simpson*

226 Circle her/him, Lord, keep harm without.
Circle her/him, Lord, keep evil without.
Circle her/him, Lord, keep strife without.
Circle her/him, Lord, keep lies without.
Circle her/him, Lord, keep hatred without.   *Ray Simpson*

A prayer for parents

227 Father of love,
accept the thanksgiving of these parents.
May their spirits, lifted to you now in humble gratitude,
always turn to you for help and strength.
Give them wisdom, tenderness and patience
to guide their child to know right from wrong. *Ray Simpson*

A prayer for parents

228 Father, may [name] and [name] be to each other
a strength in need, a comfort in sorrow,
a companion in joy.
Knit their wills together in your will,
that they may live together
in love, hope and peace
all of their days.   *Ray Simpson*

A prayer for family, godparents and friends

229 May you respect one another;
may the goodness of friendship grow in you;
may the love that covers a multitude of sins be upon you.
God's peace be with you, whatever you do;
God's light to guide you wherever you go;
God's goodness to fill you and help you to grow.
                                                     Ray Simpson

Weddings

230 Living God,
we praise you for this day of joy and celebration,
love and commitment,
nostalgia and anticipation.
For all that this day means,
we thank you.

We thank you for all A and C have shared,
and all they will share –
for the happiness they have found in each other,
and their desire today before us and you
to bear witness to that happiness.
For all that this day means,
we thank you.

We thank you for the love this service speaks of –
the love A and C have for each other,
the love of family and friends,
the love you have for us.
For all that this day means,
we thank you.

Living God,
open our hearts, we pray, to all you would say to us.
May this be a day for A and C to remember with gratitude,
the first of many days and many years of lasting fulfilment.
And may this for us all be a day
when we recognise more clearly
the greatness of your love,
and in glad thanksgiving make our response.
For all that this day means,
we thank you,
in the name of Christ we pray.

Nick Fawcett

231 God of love,
we come together on this special day
to give you thanks,
to celebrate,
and to worship.
Gracious God,
hear our prayer.

We come remembering everything
that has made this day possible –
the love that has surrounded A and C since their birth,
the experiences that have shaped their characters,
the events that have brought them together
and cemented their relationship.

Gracious God,
hear our prayer.

We come looking forward to everything the future holds –
the joys A and C will share,
the dreams they will work to fulfil,
the love that will continue to grow.
Gracious God,
hear our prayer.

We come rejoicing in everything this present moment has
to offer –
the reunion of family and friends,
the fun, laughter and happiness we share,
the joining together before you of husband and wife.
Gracious God,
hear our prayer.

God of love,
this is a precious day –
a time for thanksgiving, celebration, and worship.
Accept our praise for everything you have done,
and everything we are privileged to witness today.
And grant your blessing on all the future holds,
so that all we hope for and more besides
may be realised over the years to come.
Gracious God,
hear our prayer,
through Jesus Christ our Lord.   *Nick Fawcett*

232 Gracious God,
we are here to celebrate,
to rejoice and give thanks.
We come, not just to enjoy a special occasion,
but to seek your blessing upon a continuing journey,
a lifetime of exploration and discovery
in which we pray that love
will grow, flourish and blossom.
Meet with us now.
Be with us always.

We are here to witness an act of commitment,
a mutual pledging of vows,
a consecration of two lives woven into one relationship.
Meet with us now.
Be with us always.

We are here to praise you for the gift of love,
to thank you for the joy A and C have found in each other,
and to commit the future into your hands.
Meet with us now.
Be with us always.

Gracious God,
draw near to us in this service,
draw near to A and C,
and may your sovereign love enfold us all,
this day and for evermore.
Meet with us now.
Be with us always.
Through Jesus Christ our Lord. *Nick Fawcett*

233 Loving God,
we thank you for this special day –
this day of rejoicing, celebration, expectation
and new beginnings.
Lord of love,
hear our prayer.

We thank you for this couple –
all they mean to us,
all they mean to each other,
and all they mean to you.
Lord of love,
hear our prayer.

We thank you for bringing them together,
for the love they share,
and the life they look forward to.
Lord of love,
hear our prayer.

Enrich both them and us through being here today.
May the making of vows,
the exchanging of rings,
the reading of your word,
and the offering of our worship,
speak powerfully of the gift of human love,
and more powerfully still of your eternal love
that unfailingly encircles us.
Lord of love,
hear our prayer.

Loving God,
grant your blessing upon A and C,
so that in everything the future holds,
for better or for worse,
for richer for poorer,
in sickness and in health,
they may continue to cherish each other,
and their love continue to grow.
Grant that the closeness they feel now
may be just as real, as sure, and as special
tomorrow and in the years to come as it is today.
Lord of love,
hear our prayer,
in the name of Christ.   *Nick Fawcett*

234 Living God,
there is so much to enjoy in this day,
not simply this service now, central though it is,
but everything else that is part of this occasion:
the giving and receiving of gifts,
the taking of photographs,
the making of speeches,
the fun of the reception,
the excitement of family and friends,
the prospect of time away on honeymoon –
so much happiness,
so much laughter,
so much to celebrate.

And we thank you for it all with glad and joyful hearts.
Lord, in your love,
hear our prayer.

But we pray that through it all
you will save us from losing sight
of what this day is really all about –
your gift of love;
and not just love in the sentimental way we use that word,
but the way you understand it:
a love that is patient and kind,
never insisting on its own way,
nor arrogant, rude, irritable or resentful,
but rejoicing in truth,
bearing all things,
believing all things,
hoping all things,
enduring all things.
Lord, in your love,
hear our prayer.

Living God,
help us to enjoy this day,
celebrating every part of it enthusiastically
as your gift to us.
But help us also to remember that without love at its heart
this day would be nothing.
And so grant your blessing upon A and C,
and upon each of us in our own relationships,
so that whatever we may face
our love may continue to grow,
this day and always.
Lord, in your love,
hear our prayer,
in the name of Jesus Christ our Lord.   *Nick Fawcett*

235   Sovereign God,
       this is a day of love –
       a time of joining together,
       exchanging vows,
       uniting two lives as one.

For all that this day means,
receive our praise.

This is a day of joy –
an occasion of celebration,
laughter,
and thanksgiving.
For all that this day means,
receive our praise.

This is a day for reminiscing –
for remembering everything A and C have meant
to their loved ones over the years,
for looking back to the times we have shared with them,
and for recalling how their love for each other has grown
since they first met.
For all that this day means,
receive our praise.

This is a day for anticipation –
for looking forward to everything the future holds,
for sharing in A and C's excitement as they plan ahead,
and for rejoicing in this new chapter in their lives.
For all that this day means,
receive our praise.

This is a day for worship –
for recognising your presence here among us,
acknowledging your goodness
and asking your blessing on A and C
in the years ahead.
For all that this day means,
receive our praise.

Sovereign God,
we thank you for this special day –
put your hand upon it.
We thank you for this special couple –
put your hand on them.
We thank you for the opportunity
to share in this happy occasion –
put your hand on us.

Come now,
and make this time everything we want it to be,
and everything you can make it become.
For all that this day means,
receive our praise.
Through Jesus Christ our Lord.   *Nick Fawcett*

236   Gracious God,
we thank you for A and C,
for all they mean to each other,
and all they mean to us.
Loving Lord,
gratefully we worship you.

We thank you for the way you have brought A and
C together,
the times they have shared,
and the love that has grown between them.
And we praise you that they have reached this point
of committing themselves to each other in marriage,
pledging before you and this congregation
their desire to share their lives together,
for better, for worse,
for richer, for poorer,
in sickness and in health,
till they are parted by death.
Loving Lord,
gratefully we worship you.

We thank you for the joy that A and C feel at this moment,
and the joy we share with them;
the sense of promise and excitement
which has touched all our lives today,
and which we pray will continue for A and C
in the years ahead.
Loving Lord,
gratefully we worship you.

We thank you for everything that has led up to this day –
the moment A and C first met,
the way they have grown together,

the planning and preparation behind this service
and the reception to come,
the buying of gifts and sending of cards –
everything that helps to make this day so special.
And, above all, we thank you for your guiding hand
which makes not just this day possible, but every day,
and which is always outstretched in love,
looking to draw us to your side.
Loving Lord,
gratefully we worship you.

Gracious God,
we come today with grateful hearts,
to celebrate,
to rejoice,
and to seek your blessing on the journey
which A and C are stepping out into today.
Go with them both,
and with us all,
now and for evermore.
Loving Lord,
gratefully we worship you.
In the name of Christ.   *Nick Fawcett*

Before the start of a wedding service

237 Open our eyes to your presence.
Open our ears to your call.
Open our hearts to your love.   *Ray Simpson*

After the entrance of the bride as she stands beside the groom

238 Most powerful Spirit of God,
come down upon us and subdue us.
From heaven –
where the ordinary is made glorious
and glory seems but ordinary –
bathe us with the brilliance
of your light, like dew.   *Ray Simpson*

Before the vows

239 May the Father take you
in his fragrant clasp of love,
in every up and every down of your life.   *Ray Simpson*

240 The love and affection of God be with you.
The love and affection of the angels
be with you.
The love and affection of the saints in heaven
be with you.
The love and affection of your friends on Earth
be with you,
to guard you,
to cherish you,
to bring you to your eternal fulfilment.   *Ray Simpson*

Joining hands after the vows

241 May you be bound
with unbreakable bonds of love to one another.
May you be bound
with unbreakable bonds of love to your God.
May your love for each other
reflect the love of your Maker, Saviour and Guide:
the Three of Limitless Love.   *Ray Simpson*

A bridal blessing after the vows

242 May the Father take you in his fragrant clasp of love.
May the Virgin Mary's Son guide you
through the maze of life.
May the generous Spirit release forgiving love within you.
Hour by hour, by day and by night, in joy and in failure,
may each man and each woman who is a saint in heaven
urge you on to complete your course.   *Ray Simpson*

243 God's own presence with you stay,
Jesus to shield you in the fray,
Spirit to protect you from all ill,
Trinity there guiding you still.

On sea or land, in ebb or flow,
God be with you wherever you go;
in flow or ebb, on land or sea,
God's great might your protecting be.   *Ray Simpson*

244 May you share hopes and dreams,
but also walk through hard times hand in hand.
May your love for each other keep burning bright,
but if ever it flickers low may Jesus,
the Eternal Fire Kindler, light up the fire again.
In your old age, as now when you are younger,
may you be best friends,
and give each other room to be yourselves.   *Ray Simpson*

(The words in italics may be used as an optional response by the couple)

245 Gracious God,
we are here to celebrate your love,
and rejoice in your great faithfulness.
You have been always good to us,
always true,
always by our side,
and we praise you for it.
Receive our praise,
in the name of Christ.

Day by day you have held us close,
sharing with us in the good times and bad,
our surest and dearest friend,
and we thank you for it.
Receive our praise,
in the name of Christ.

Gracious God,
we are here to celebrate your gift of love,
the love that A and C have shared over so many years,
the faithfulness they have shown to each other –
the closeness that has grown between them.
Receive our praise,
in the name of Christ.

We are here to celebrate how you have sustained them,
through joy and sorrow,
hopes and fears,
trials and temptations,
good and bad.
Receive our praise,
in the name of Christ.

Gracious God,
we are here to celebrate,
with you,
with A and C,
and with one another.
Speak to us through the vows renewed in this service,
of the love you have for us,
and help us to pledge our love in return to you.
Receive our praise,
in the name of Christ.
Nick Fawcett

246   Eternal God,
we come today to celebrate the gift of love –
your love for us,
and the love of A and C for each other.
You have blessed us,
and we thank you.

We thank you that though all else may change,
though heaven and earth may pass away,
your love continues unchanging,
constant and dependable,
always the same,
always certain.
You have blessed us,
and we thank you.

We thank you for the way you have been with A and C
throughout their lives –
the way you brought them together,
the way you have guided them,
nurtured and enriched their relationship,
and blessed them and their loved ones.

You have blessed us,
and we thank you.

We thank you for their commitment to each other,
to their family,
to us,
and to Christ.
You have blessed us,
and we thank you.

Go with them now,
watch over them,
and grant them many more years
of health and happiness together,
until that day when you unite them and all your people
in your everlasting kingdom
and the joy of your unchanging presence.
You have blessed us,
and we thank you,
in the name of Christ.

Nick Fawcett

247   Gracious God,
we praise you for your gift of love –
that most precious of gifts which endures beyond all others,
bearing all things,
believing all things
and hoping all things.
We rejoice that it is a love such as this
which we come to celebrate today.
Receive our thanks,
and accept our worship.

We thank you for the joy that comes
from two lives truly being shared,
from two people becoming one,
each complementing and enriching the other,
each helping love to grow.
Receive our thanks,
and accept our worship.

We recall before you everything A and C have shared
across the years –
the joys and sorrows,
hopes and fears,
triumphs and disappointments,
pleasure and pain –
and we thank you that they have shared those times together,
offering mutual support, strength and encouragement.
Receive our thanks,
and accept our worship.

We celebrate everything their love has meant to others –
the inspiration it has given,
happiness it has contributed to,
security it has provided,
and example it has offered to family and friends alike.
Receive our thanks,
and accept our worship.

We acknowledge your love which has been a constant thread
throughout their relationship –
your presence which has always been with them,
your hand upon them today,
and the assurance that you will continue to bless them
in the years ahead,
whatever life may bring.
Receive our thanks,
and accept our worship.

So now we bring you this day of celebration
and this act of recommitment,
acknowledging with gratitude the good times enjoyed,
and looking forward with expectation to the joys yet to come.
Receive our thanks,
and accept our worship.
Through Jesus Christ our Lord.   *Nick Fawcett*

(This prayer is for those who have experienced difficulties in their marriage and who wish to remake their vows as a symbol of their desire to start again)

248 Living God,
you tell us that love is patient and kind,
not envious or boastful, arrogant or rude.
You say that love is not irritable or resentful,
insisting on its own way and rejoicing in wrongdoing,
but, instead, it rejoices in the truth,
bearing all things,
believing all things,
hoping all things,
enduring all things.
We confess that our love isn't always like that,
all too often falling far short of such an ideal.
It is sometimes shaken,
and, on occasions, tested to breaking point.
Yet we come today acknowledging our weakness
and asking for another chance to love as you love us.
Receive what we are,
and direct what we shall be.

We come with A and C today,
acknowledging mistakes that have been made,
errors of judgement and lack of thought –
the words that shouldn't have been spoken
and those that should but never were;
the deeds that shouldn't have been contemplated
and those we failed even to consider –
and we ask your forgiveness for them all.
Receive what we are,
and direct what we shall be.

Give to A and C the ability to start afresh –
to put the past behind them,
learning its lessons yet allowing its wounds to heal –
and help each of us in turn to learn likewise,
open to others' point of view,
ready to forgive and forget,
always looking to see the best rather than the worst.

Receive what we are
and direct what we shall be.

Living God,
we believe you are a God who makes all things new,
constantly restoring and recreating,
and so we come to share in this act of rededication,
this renewal of vows and affirming of commitment.
Move within A and C,
work within us,
and fill each one of us with your love,
in body, mind and spirit.
Receive what we are,
and direct what we shall be.
Through Jesus Christ our Lord.   *Nick Fawcett*

Blessing
249   A and C,
may the grace of God always surround you,
enriching your lives and nurturing your love,
seasoning your words and shaping your actions,
uniting you in times of trial,
supporting you in moments of sorrow,
and bringing you lasting joy and enduring fulfilment.
May the Lord be with you,
his hands below,
his arms around,
and his Spirit within you,
and may he lead you this and every day,
as you travel together along life's chequered path.
In the name of Christ.   *Nick Fawcett*

250   When we have buried your insight beneath falsehoods,
when we have insulated ourselves
from being vulnerable to others,
when we have been closed to your renewing of our minds,
have mercy on us.
Break through our resistance.
Open our hearts to love.   *Ray Simpson*

251 Source of our being and goal of our longing,
give us wisdom to harvest our life
and find the wholeness of memory.
We bring to you abandoned areas of our lives.
Heal our wounds, keep bright the flame.
Kindle in us the memory of love and discovery. *Ray Simpson*

252 Eternal Wisdom, firstborn of creation,
you emptied yourself of power
and became foolish for our sake.
You laboured with us on the cross
and became Wisdom's crown.
At this table we lay down our proud pretensions
and become one with you.
We pray for
the oppressed and powerless peoples of the world,
that in their powerlessness
they may discover Wisdom's Way. *Ray Simpson*

253 Warm-winged Spirit, brooding over creation,
draw forth the divine beauty in every person on Earth:
in women who feel degraded
and in men who abuse their role;
in children who are orphaned
and in the disabled who are frail. *Ray Simpson*

254 Wisdom, breathing through all creation,
you planted your likeness in us.
As a mother tenderly gathers her children
you embraced a people as your own. *Ray Simpson*

255 Heavenly Father,
we offer you our praise and thanksgiving
for [number] years together;
for all the joys we have shared;
for our friends and family (especially our children [names]).
May they always know of our love for them,
and grant us wisdom in the years to come. *Ray Simpson*

256 Forgive us
when we grumble about the married state;
when we complain we haven't enough money;
when we are quarrelsome
and won't admit we are wrong;
and when we find fault with each other.   *Ray Simpson*

257 O God,
we confess our ingratitude for your goodness
and our selfishness in using your gifts.
We ask you to forgive us and to use us to your glory.
                                                 Ray Simpson

258 Heavenly Father,
we offer you our souls and bodies,
our thoughts and words and deeds,
our love for one another,
our past and our future.
Unite our will in your will.
May we and our children
grow together in love and peace
all the days of our life,
through Jesus Christ our Lord.   *Ray Simpson*

259 The Lord renew his place in your lives,
give you grace to complete
the work in you he has begun.
The Lord bless you and watch over you
and be gracious to you;
the Lord look kindly on you
and give you peace now and always.   *Ray Simpson*

Funerals

260 We are here to express sorrow that a life is ended,
to give thanks for a life well-lived.
We are here grieving that a life is over,
but rejoicing that life eternal has just begun.

We are here conscious of separation,
yet confident we shall meet again.
We are here remembering what has been,
and looking forward to what shall be.
We are here to pay tribute to all AB has meant to us,
to remind ourselves of all he/she means to God.
We are here to entrust someone we have greatly loved
to his eternal keeping,
and to entrust ourselves to the same God
who so greatly loves us.
Listen then to words of Scripture and tribute,
bring your pain, your shock and sadness,
offer to God this time of worship,
and receive the comfort he longs to give you,
in the name of Christ.   *Nick Fawcett*

261   Loving God,
we come today struggling for words to express our feelings,
lost for words to express our thanks
for all AB has meant to us.
We come with sorrow as we think of our loss,
with gratitude as we recall the person A has been,
with praise as we remember
all you have done through him/her,
with faith as we commit both A and ourselves
to your eternal care.

Loving God,
draw near to us as we draw near to you.
Speak to us through the words of Scripture,
through our prayers,
through all we shall share,
so that, believing in the Gospel and trusting in Christ,
we may receive the comfort, peace and strength
you long to give us,
and find hope in this life,
and the life to come.
Through Jesus Christ our Lord.   *Nick Fawcett*

262 We have come together in the presence of God,
and in the name of Christ.
We come with sorrow,
but also with hope;
to express loss,
but also to give thanks;
to recognise death,
but also to celebrate life;
to look back at all that has been,
but also to look forward to all that is yet to be.
Come then in faith, for God is here –
the God who has promised that, in life or in death,
he is with us,
the God who gives all who truly believe
the assurance of his eternal blessing.   *Nick Fawcett*

263 Lord,
someone we have loved has died,
someone special to us,
precious,
irreplaceable.
And we know there are no words we can say at this moment
to express what we are feeling,
no words that can alleviate our sorrow
or take away our pain.
So we come today simply to bring you the grief,
the shock and the pain,
the emptiness, the anger and the despair,
the loneliness, the fear and the uncertainty
which overwhelms us at this time.
We come bringing those honestly before you,
and asking for strength in this time of darkness.
Hold on to us,
even when we find it hard to hold on to you.
Be very near,
even when we feel you to be very far.
Support us in the days ahead,
and grant the comfort you have promised,
until the time finally comes when we can look back

not just with pain but thanksgiving –
not just with sorrow but with joy.
Through Jesus Christ our Lord,
the Resurrection and the Life!   *Nick Fawcett*

264   Loving God,
      we come today to express our sorrow but also our joy,
      to remember but also to anticipate,
      to mourn but also to give thanks.
      Lord, in your mercy,
      hear our prayer.

      We come with gratitude in our hearts
      for all AB has meant to us,
      for all he/she continues to mean to us,
      for all he/she will always mean to you.
      Lord, in your mercy,
      hear our prayer.

      We come to acknowledge a life well-lived,
      and in faith to commit both A and ourselves
      to your eternal care.
      Lord, in your mercy,
      hear our prayer.

      Loving God,
      draw near to us as we draw near to you.
      Speak to us through the words of Scripture and tribute,
      through our hymns and prayers,
      through all we share,
      so that believing in the Good News of Christ,
      and trusting in him,
      we may receive the comfort he promises,
      the peace that passes all understanding,
      and the assurance of everlasting life,
      through Jesus Christ our Lord.
      Lord, in your mercy,
      hear our prayer,
      for in his name we pray.   *Nick Fawcett*

265 Gracious God,
we thank you for the person AB has been to us.
We thank you for his/her love and friendship,
honesty and integrity,
kindness and thoughtfulness,
wisdom and humility.
We thank you for his/her faithful service in so much,
his/her dedication at work,
to his/her family,
to our church,
to Christ.
We thank you for his/her faith,
his/her commitment,
his/her discipleship,
his/her witness to the love of Christ.

Gracious God,
we thank you that A has enriched our lives,
that he/she has brought happiness to many,
that he/she has earned our love and respect,
that he/she is one we will truly mourn.
But most of all we thank you that our confidence,
our hope and our trust now is real,
for A has run the race and kept the faith
and is now with you and all your people
in your heavenly kingdom.
Watch over A and bless him/her,
until that time when we shall meet again,
and live together in the light of your everlasting love,
through Jesus Christ our Lord.   *Nick Fawcett*

266 Living God,
we bring you our thanks for AB,
for the person he/she has been,
for all he/she has meant in so many innumerable ways.
We thank you for his/her warmth and love,
his/her enthusiasm and zest for life,
his/her courage and cheerfulness,
his/her many interests and abilities.

We thank you for all the happiness A has brought
to those around him/her,
and especially to his/her family.
We thank you for all the special times shared;
those moments which will live on in our minds
as enduring memories,
bringing pain in their remembering but also joy.

We thank you for the convictions A has held
throughout his/her life,
those things he/she has believed in and worked for.
And we thank you for the faith
which has given him/her such support,
and which offers us the same support now.

Give us confidence in the victory over death
you have won through Christ,
certainty that your kingdom will come,
conviction that nothing will finally separate us from
your love,
and so may we find strength not just for today,
but for tomorrow and all that the future holds.
In the name of Christ we ask it.   *Nick Fawcett*

267   Gracious God,
we entrust AB into your everlasting care,
and, as we do so, we thank you again
for all he/she has meant to us,
for the person he/she has been,
for the service he/she has offered
and for the contribution he/she has made to our lives.
Gratefully we come:
lovingly we give thanks.

We thank you for everything A has meant to his/her family,
to colleagues and friends,
to us here today,
and we thank you for all he/she continues to mean to you
as well as to us.
Gratefully we come:
lovingly we give thanks.

We thank you for A's achievements
which we can look back on with pride,
the challenges faced,
the obstacles overcome,
the successes won,
the potential fulfilled.
Gratefully we come:
lovingly we give thanks.

We thank you for the experiences we have been
through together,
the love and friendship we have shared,
the qualities and characteristics which made A special to us.
Gratefully we come:
lovingly we give thanks.

We thank you for A's faith*,
his/her commitment to Christ,
faithful discipleship and personal experience of your love.
Gratefully we come:
lovingly we give thanks.

We thank you for all we owe to A,
for the innumerable ways in which he/she enriched
our lives,
and for the memories we will always have
as a lasting tribute and enduring legacy.
Gratefully we come:
lovingly we give thanks.

Gracious God,
we come in hope and confidence,
trusting in your promise,
and assured of your gracious purpose,
and in that faith we entrust both A and ourselves
into your gracious keeping,
now and for all eternity.
Gratefully we come:
lovingly we give thanks.
Through Jesus Christ our Lord.   *Nick Fawcett*

* Omit this stanza if the deceased professed no Christian faith

268 Loving God,
we praise you that on this day of mourning,
and at this time of pain,
we can come still with hope in our hearts
and thanksgiving on our lips,
for we know that what seems like the end
with you is a new beginning.
Christ has died.
Christ has risen.
Thanks be to God!

We praise you that in Jesus
you experienced not just our life but our death –
that you endured the darkness of Gethsemane,
the agony of the cross,
and the finality of the tomb;
and you emerged victorious,
triumphant over everything that would keep us from you,
conquering death itself.
Christ has died.
Christ has risen.
Thanks be to God!

We thank you that where the world saw only defeat,
you brought victory;
that in despair and sorrow, you brought joy;
that in darkness and doubt, you brought light;
that nothing is able to overshadow your love,
no power able to withstand your purpose.
Christ has died.
Christ has risen.
Thanks be to God!

Loving God,
we praise you that we can come today
not to close a book but to end a chapter,
not to say goodbye
but rather to bid a friend farewell for now.
In that confidence we entrust A into your eternal care,
knowing that the love which surrounds him/her
surrounds us all,
now and for evermore.

Christ has died.
Christ has risen.
Thanks be to God! *Nick Fawcett*

269 Loving God,
you have promised that those who mourn shall be
comforted.
So we pray now for each of us here today,
bringing before you the sorrow we all feel at this moment.
Lord, in your mercy,
hear our prayer.

We pray especially for A's family,
in their shock and grief,
their pain and loneliness,
the turmoil of emotions which death inevitably brings
to those left behind.
Lord, in your mercy,
hear our prayer.

We pray for all those who counted A as a friend,
those in this church,
those who worked with A,
who lived near to him/her,
who shared his/her hobbies and interests –
all those whose lives were, in different ways,
touched by A's presence.
Lord, in your mercy,
hear our prayer.

Loving God,
we bring before you now our sense of emptiness,
separation and sorrow.
Give us your support as we struggle
to come to terms with our loss.
Give strength to face the days ahead.
Give courage when life seems dark.
Give hope when the future seems without purpose.
Lord, in your mercy,
hear our prayer.

Help us to know that your love for A and for us
continues beyond death,
that you are with us in this moment and always,
and may that knowledge bring comfort and hope
today and in the days ahead.
Lord, in your mercy,
hear our prayer,
in the name of Christ.   *Nick Fawcett*

270   Loving God,
you tell us to look forward to a day
when your kingdom shall come
and your will be done;
a new age when there will be no more suffering,
sorrow or death;
a place where there will be no more mourning and weeping,
every tear wiped away from our eyes.
Help us to find comfort in your love.

We thank you for that promise,
and we look forward to that time,
but we pray also for your help now,
for today our grief is all too painful,
and the fact of death an all too stark reality.
Help us to find comfort in your love.

So we ask you to reach out to us
and to all whose lives have been enriched
by A's presence –
family,
friends,
neighbours,
colleagues –
each so much the poorer for A's passing.
Help us to find comfort in your love.

Loving God,
reach out now into the darkness of this moment,
the blackness of our sorrow,
and grant your light which nothing can overcome,

your peace that defies understanding,
and your hope which will never be extinguished.
Help us to find comfort in your love,
through Jesus Christ our Lord.   *Nick Fawcett*

271 Loving God,
as we wrestle now with our grief,
we are reminded of all who have lost loved ones,
whose lives have been touched by tragedy,
and who are overwhelmed by sorrow.
Lord, in your mercy,
hear our prayer.

We pray for them in their shock, hurt and bewilderment.
We lift before you their sense of desolation and despair,
their feelings of numbness and emptiness,
their aching hearts which see just a blank void
where so much joy used to be.
Lord, in your mercy,
hear our prayer.

We pray for each one of us here today
and especially for those closest to A;
for (enter names as appropriate).
Reach out and encircle them in your loving arms.
Grant them the comfort you have promised to all who mourn,
your peace that passes understanding,
your light that reaches into the darkest places of life
and beyond into the darkness of death.
Lord, in your mercy,
hear our prayer.

Loving God,
may the hope of the gospel,
the experience of your love,
and the support of family and friends
bring the help that is needed at this time;
the strength to endure sorrow in all its intensity
and to face death in all its apparent finality,
yet ultimately to look forward in faith,
knowing that, in Christ, nothing can finally separate us
from you or from those we love.

Lord, in your mercy,
hear our prayer.
We ask it for his name's sake.   *Nick Fawcett*

272   Go to your eternal home of welcome,
      our loved companion.
      Go into the sleep of Jesus,
      the restoring sleep of Jesus,
      the young sleep of Jesus.
      Go into the kiss and the peace and glory of Jesus;
      into the arms of the Jesus of blessings;
      into the generous Christ with his hands around you;
      drawing near to the Trinity,
      freed from your pains,
      pardoned from your sins,
      Christ beside you
      bringing peace to your mind.   *Ray Simpson*

273   May you who were baptised as
      [deceased person's baptismal names]
      now be immersed in the life of God.
      Into the presence of the Creator we immerse you.
      Into the presence of the Saviour we immerse you.
      Into the presence of the Spirit we immerse you. *Ray Simpson*

274   Lord of the Great Passage,
      you hold a crown ready in your hand.
      If I trust in my own will
      I cannot receive it.
      I trust in you alone
      and I am eager to come to you.   *Ray Simpson*

275   Holy God, holy and mighty,
      you alone are Creator,
      you alone are Saviour of all,
      you alone are immortal.   *Ray Simpson*

276 We are mortal,
formed from the earth, returning to the earth;
for you ordained
that we should come from dust and go to dust.
Yet through Christ you ordained also
that with our tears at the dark night of parting
should be mingled the Alleluias
of the glory that pierces the gloom from beyond.
So as we remember the shadows,
and as we linger with our precious memories
may we feel your presence.
May we be touched by your hope.
May we be changed by your glory. *Ray Simpson*

277 We arise today
in the strength of the mighty Creator,
in the strength of the rising Saviour,
in the strength of the life-giving Spirit,
in the strength of the mighty Three
whose love is One.

We arise today
in the strength of the angels and archangels,
in the strength of the prophets and apostles,
in the strength of the martyrs and saints.

We arise today
in the strength of heaven and Earth,
in the strength of sun and moon,
in the strength of fire and wind.

We arise today
in the strength of Christ's birth and baptism,
in the strength of Christ's death and rising,
in the strength of Christ's judgement to come. *Ray Simpson*

278 Strength-giver, may your fibre grow in us.
Fortifier, may your praises swell in us.
Indweller, may your presence dwell in us. *Ray Simpson*

279 You led your people by a cloud;
lead us by your Spirit now.
You lit your people by a fire;
light us by your Spirit now.   *Ray Simpson*

280 O Spirit, be free in us.
Let us not bind you through fear
of where your disturbing power will lead.
Burst through these brittle shells;
shake us to the foundations;
strip us to the core
which is our essence and your love.
Echoes an anonymous prayer   *Ray Simpson*

CPSIA information can be obtained
at www.ICGtesting.com
Printed in the USA
JSHW042242200520
5809JS00001B/5

9 781506 460178